Public Expenditures and Taxation

NATIONAL BUREAU OF ECONOMIC RESEARCH

General Series 96

Economic Research: Retrospect and Prospect

PUBLIC EXPENDITURES
AND TAXATION

Fiftieth Anniversary Colloquium IV

NATIONAL BUREAU OF ECONOMIC RESEARCH
NEW YORK 1972

Distributed by COLUMBIA UNIVERSITY PRESS
NEW YORK AND LONDON

Relation of National Bureau Directors to Publications
Reporting Proceedings of the Fiftieth Anniversary Colloquia

Since the present volume is a record of colloquium proceedings, it has been exempted from the rules governing submission of manuscripts to, and critical review by, the Board of Directors of the National Bureau.
(Resolution adopted July 6, 1948, as revised
November 21, 1949, and April 20, 1968)

Prefatory Note

This volume of the Fiftieth Anniversary Series contains the proceedings of Public Expenditures and Taxation, a colloquium held in Washington, D.C., on December 2, 1970. We are indebted to Hal Lary and to those members of the Bureau's Board of Directors who served on the committee to plan and coordinate the session: Francis M. Boddy, Emilio Collado, Otto Eckstein, Thomas D. Flynn, Walter W. Heller, and Jacob Viner. We are also grateful to Gnomi Gouldin, Virginia Meltzer, Ester Moskowitz, and Ruth Ridler, who prepared the manuscript for publication.

With pride and pleasure, we dedicate this volume to the memory of Harold M. Groves, whose contributions to the field of public finance were legion. Through his lifelong empirical research, his lucid and insightful writings, and the outstanding "crop" of Wisconsin Ph.D.'s who bear his stamp, he left an enduring legacy to the profession. Professor Groves was a valued member of the National Bureau's Board of Directors, on which he served by appointment of the University of Wisconsin from 1939 through 1968, at which time he assumed emeritus status until his death on December 4, 1969. He was Chairman of the Board during 1961 and 1962 and one of his last Bureau activities concerned helping to plan the Public Expenditures and Taxation colloquium. His generous advice and assistance helped to mold the session, and many of the ideas which emerged during the discussion bear his imprint.

Fiftieth Anniversary Colloquium Series

To commemorate its fiftieth anniversary the National Bureau of Economic Research sponsored a series of colloquia to explore the effects of pending and anticipated policy issues on future research priorities for areas of long-standing Bureau concern. As a basis for the panel and audience discussions, economists specializing in the subject area prepared papers in which they reviewed relevant research advances through time and presented their opinions for the direction of future effort. These papers, and in some instances edited transcripts of panelists' comments, appear as part of the National Bureau's Fiftieth Anniversary publications series. Papers developed for the colloquia and publications series and participants in the program included:

THE BUSINESS CYCLE TODAY
September 24, 1970—New York City

Moderators:
>Morning session: Paul A. Samuelson
>Afternoon session: F. Thomas Juster

Presentations:
>"Dating American Growth Cycles"　　　　　　　*Ilse Mintz*
>"The 'Recession' of 1969–1970"　　　　*Solomon Fabricant*
>"The Cyclical Behavior of Prices"　　　　*Geoffrey H. Moore*
>"Forecasting Economic Conditions: The Record and the Prospect"
>　　　　　　　　　　　　　　　　　　*Victor Zarnowitz*
>"Econometric Model Simulations and the Cyclical Characteristics of the U.S. Economy"　　　　　　*Victor Zarnowitz*
>"A Study of Discretionary and Nondiscretionary Monetary and Fiscal Policies in the Context of Stochastic Macroeconometric Models"　　　　　*Yoel Haitovsky and Neil Wallace*

Panelists:
Morning session: Otto Eckstein, Henry C. Wallich
Afternoon session: Bert G. Hickman, Arthur M. Okun

FINANCE AND CAPITAL MARKETS
October 22, 1970—New York City

Moderator: Robert V. Roosa

Presentation:
"Finance and Capital Markets"   *John Lintner*

Panelists: William J. Baumol, Sidney Homer, James J. O'Leary

A ROUNDTABLE ON POLICY ISSUES AND RESEARCH OPPORTUNITIES IN INDUSTRIAL ORGANIZATION
November 5, 1970—Chicago, Illinois

Moderator: Victor R. Fuchs

Presentations:
"Industrial Organization: Boxing the Compass"
James W. McKie
"Antitrust Enforcement and the Modern Corporation"
Oliver E. Williamson
"Issues in the Study of Industrial Organization in a Regime of Rapid Technical Change"   *Richard R. Nelson*
"Industrial Organization: A Proposal for Research"
Ronald H. Coase

PUBLIC EXPENDITURES AND TAXATION
December 2, 1970—Washington, D.C.

Moderator: Walter W. Heller

Presentation:
"Quantitative Research in Taxation and Government Expenditure"
Carl S. Shoup
Panelists: James M. Buchanan, Richard R. Musgrave

ECONOMIC GROWTH
December 10, 1970—San Francisco, California

Moderator: R. Aaron Gordon

Presentation:
"Is Growth Obsolete?"
William D. Nordhaus and James Tobin

Panelists: Moses Abramovitz, Robin C. O. Matthews

HUMAN RESOURCES
May 13, 1971—Atlanta, Georgia

Moderator: Gary S. Becker

Presentation:
"Human Capital: Policy Issues and Research Opportunities"
Theodore W. Schultz

Panelists: Alice M. Rivlin, Gerald S. Somers

THE FUTURE OF ECONOMIC RESEARCH
April 23, 1971—South Brookline, Massachusetts

Presentation:

"Quantitative Economic Research: Trends and Problems"

Simon Kuznets

Contents

FOREWORD   Edward K. Smith   xv

QUANTITATIVE RESEARCH IN TAXATION
    AND GOVERNMENT EXPENDITURE
                                    Carl S. Shoup   1

DISCUSSION   61

Foreword

Every discipline is subject to having too much claimed for it by its practitioners. Public finance may be no exception, but a reading of this volume will lead many to conclude that the subject matter is so broad, up to and including general equilibrium models, that many of its practitioners have claimed too little rather than too much for it. Agendas for research are revealing, for the larger the agenda, the greater the likelihood that the subject matter impinges on, or is inclusive of, other disciplines. This is as true of a subdiscipline of a science as of the science itself. A cynic might charge that agendas are large because they are directly proportionate to the ignorance expressed. A more realistic view, and one to which most of us would subscribe, is that, as a discipline expands its knowledge, it simultaneously increases the area of new and unanswered questions. The expansion of knowledge increases the penumbra of the unknown at the frontiers, for the frontiers have widened.

The essential impression one gets from this National Bureau of Economic Research Fiftieth Anniversary Colloquium is that the agenda for quantitative research in taxation and government expenditures has greatly widened and that both the new and the old questions need to be probed more deeply. In the social sciences such a conclusion is not unexpected. To some, feelings of doubt and uncertainty also enter. To others, the paradigms have been or will need to be modified; the subject matter is not now what it was thirty or more years ago. The "tired topics" must give way to the new.

This colloquium, dedicated to the late Harold Groves, a distinguished practitioner of the discipline who was long associated with the National Bureau, called upon Carl Shoup, of Columbia University and the National Bureau, to review the field and suggest an agenda for future research. Shoup restricted his review to quantitative research, a restriction that excludes theoretical contributions unaccompanied by quantitative information. Shoup uses the term quantitative, rather than empirical, because "few public finance studies of facts and figures formulated empirical statements in the sense of refutable hypotheses subject to testing by appeal to the facts." The reader will discover that while such a restriction greatly limits, it by no means denudes, the subject at hand. The agenda for research is still larger than the resources available would permit us to exploit.

Shoup examines two tax topics at length: the distribution of taxation by income classes, and the shifting and incidence of taxation. He summarizes many others, chiefly in terms of the present state of quantitative knowledge. These include effects of taxes on investment and business behavior and on the supply of labor; the excess burden of taxation; and time series and cross-section studies of tax system characteristics. Another section of his paper examines government expenditures as they have been researched to discover "laws" of expenditures, government services as outputs, and efficiency of expenditures.

Shoup appraises the need and prospects for quantitative research and possible outlets for such work. The National Bureau's reentry into the public finance field on a fairly large scale is predicted, with emphasis on the closed model, e.g., studies of tax substitutions. The author is aware that there may be some delay, for "even the simplest of such projects are likely to prove too much for any small group of individual scholars . . . on their own." Certainly economic research has suffered from the inadequate scale of individual investigations. Shoup's hope that the future will be different is shared by his coworkers.

In another section Shoup reviews the impact of past studies on the formulation of policy, and the possible policy impact that may be envisioned for the future. He concludes that for distribution studies, the policy impacts have been negligible, perhaps because policy makers felt that too many institutional restraints had to be overcome. Further studies will have to show what happens to the distribution of income under postulated tax changes along with imputation of benefits from government services and subsidy payments. Subsidies seem "to have been subject to very little serious quantitative analysis in terms of incidence." On the other hand, there have been many studies of the impact of tax changes by alternative programs. They have had a substantial role in policy making, but unfortunately most of them are produced within the government and remain unpublished. Such studies have neglected the *incidence* of taxation, however.

Richard Musgrave and James Buchanan are the discussants of Shoup's paper. Professor Buchanan feels that traditional public finance has been transformed into "one of the most exciting areas in political economy," for "our paradigms have been modified" and today public finance is "public economics." Here we see the tendency to claim much for a discipline, as I commented earlier. Consequently, Buchanan does not think Shoup has included enough in his review, and feels he should have excluded some of the "tired topics." Institutionalists are recalled to duty, especially to bring a greater degree of realism to econometric models. On the whole, Buchanan thinks Shoup has led us down the wrong path.

Professor Musgrave is willing to let the flowers bloom. Many paths can and should be tried. Large models may bring disillusionment, but the future lies in econometric work. Both big and small projects can be productive. We need to work on the analysis of bureaucracy, as Buchanan wants, as well as of tax incidence, as Shoup advises. We need also to measure the fiscal capacities and needs of various jurisdictions, the incentive effects of negative income taxation, and the substitution of value added taxes for corporate taxes.

The research agenda grows larger. The reader may add (or subtract) his own topics for investigation as he reads this volume. It is to be hoped that he will find new insights for his own agenda, choosing his own path, and no doubt increasing the breadth and depth of that which we call public finance. Walter Heller, our moderator, called it a "vast unfinished business." That it is. In the end, Professor Buchanan withdrew the word "tired."

I opened the session by introducing Walter Heller to our Washington audience. The colloquium closed with a dinner address on revenue sharing by the Hon. Paul A. Volcker, Under Secretary of the Treasury for Monetary Affairs.

EDWARD K. SMITH
Vice President

Public Expenditures and Taxation

Quantitative Research in Taxation and Government Expenditure

Carl S. Shoup
Columbia University

I. INTRODUCTION

This paper deals with certain areas and types of research in the fields of taxation and public expenditure. To make the undertaking practicable, the coverage has been limited. Broad macro issues concerned with fiscal policy for full employment, growth, external and internal price equilibrium, and the like, are excluded. Moreover, the discussion is restricted to quantitative research, and hence does not cover theoretical contributions unaccompanied by quantitative information: for example, Pigou's *A Study in Public Finance,* Musgrave's *The Theory of Public Finance,* and Buchanan's *The Demand and Supply of Public Goods.*

Quantitative rather than *empirical* is the term chosen, in order to indicate that, at least until very recently, few public finance studies of facts and figures formulated empirical statements in the sense of refutable hypotheses subject to testing by appeal to the facts. Rather, the facts have been used to suggest hypotheses that have not generally been tested by appeal to another set of data.[1]

The present survey excludes all mere compilations of quantitative descriptions, however essential they may be, if they are not accompanied by a detailed attempt at interpretation.

A choice had to be made whether to cover the main topics within the field delimited with about the same intensity, or to select some one or two parts of the field for special attention, while presenting a type of

[1] The distinction drawn here is that made in introductory textbooks: "One must be very careful to distinguish between the test of a preexisting theory and the use of observations to suggest a new and still-to-be tested theory." Edward J. Kane, *Economic Statistics and Econometrics.* New York, Harper and Row, 1968, p. 29.

Note: I am indebted to Hal B. Lary and David K. Stout for comments on an earlier draft of this paper.

summary for others. The latter course has been adopted, the topics selected for intensive examination of quantitative research being the distribution of taxation by income classes, and the shifting and incidence of taxation. These two are, of course, closely related; but, as will be seen, it has been possible to work in the former area by means of assumptions concerning the latter one—assumptions grounded, in part, on what the quantitative studies in shifting and incidence had revealed.

This decision was based on the importance of demonstrating: (1) the considerable amount of effort that normally has to be devoted to such a task (involving a fairly long period of time and a number of individuals) before agreement is reached on the details of technique to be employed, and apparent conflicts in answers arrived at by different investigators are either resolved or set aside for still further study; and (2) the increasing awareness, as the work proceeds, of just what question it is that is being answered. This, at least in the first case (distribution of taxes by income groups), is seen to be far narrower than initially supposed, though still quite important for policy purposes. The cumulative effect of incremental contributions to technique, the puzzlement aroused by initial misunderstandings, the methods developed for partial resolution of disagreements, and the like, can be appreciated only by working through an amount of detail that, if presented for all the chief topics in this field, would make the present paper far too long. Moreover, it is a task for which probably no one person in public finance is fitted.

The remaining topics, labeled II-C through III-J, are discussed chiefly in terms of the present state of quantitative knowledge.

Part IV offers a few observations in addition to—or in summary of—statements in Parts II and III with respect to future trends in quantitative research in taxation and governmental expenditure.

Part V attempts a broader, looser analysis of the role of quantitative studies in these fields in formulation of public policy.

It will be seen that even the list of topics that are treated but briefly (II-C through III-J) excludes many sectors in which important quantitative studies have been made. In particular, the tax effects that are covered in this list are chiefly those that directly concern the business world, rather than households.[2] This somewhat arbitrary selection would

---

[2] Consequently, among the many significant quantitative studies that are not covered here, are some of those published recently by The Brookings Institution, including *Economic Behavior of the Affluent,* by Robin Barlow, Harvey E. Brazer, and James N. Morgan (1966); *Alternative Approaches to Capital Gains Taxation,*

not have been acceptable had the aim of the present paper been encyclopedic. As it stands, however, the main issues of quantitative analysis in taxation and government expenditure seem well enough exemplified by the topics that have been included.

II. TAXATION

A. Distribution of Taxation by Income Levels or Classes, or Other Categories

The most popular quantitative exercise in public finance has been to distribute taxation by income classes. A few of such studies have included estimates of the distribution of benefits from government services, but they have been so rough as to be rather uninteresting, except, perhaps, the Adler study (see footnote 16 below). Distributions of taxation by family size are sometimes made; other types of distribution are rare.

Any one tax-distribution table, taken by itself, is of limited significance since—for reasons to be adduced below—it does not really say what it seems to say. Studies of two or more alternative tax systems do say something quite useful; it is meaningful to think of an existing tax system being supplanted by another, while it is meaningless to think of an existing tax system being replaced by nothing.

In these tax-distribution studies, one of two techniques has been employed: the typical-family technique or the total-tax-bill technique.

The typical-family technique uses the tax law, but no tax collection data. Given a family's consumption and income levels and patterns, the tax rates can be applied, with appropriate assumptions about incidence as contrasted with initial impact, to yield a tax bill for that family. Similar data are given for other similarly specified families at other income levels.

In contrast, the total-tax-bill technique uses tax collection data and does not require information on tax rates, tax bases, and the like. It allocates total personal income-tax revenue to income groups: for example, $2 billion of income tax revenue is ascertained to be paid by all taxpayers (married or single, and regardless of number of children) of families with incomes from above ten-thousand to twelve-thousand dol-

by Martin David (1968); *Federal Tax Treatment of the Family,* by Harold M. Groves (1963); *Trusts and Estate Taxation,* by Gerald R. Jantscher (1967); and *Consumer Responses to Income Increases,* by George Katona and Eva Mueller (1968).

lars, their aggregate income being $30 billion. Total tobacco-tax reve-
nue is allocated among income groups under assumptions, or studies,
of relative amounts of tobacco consumed in the several income groups,
and assumptions about the degree of forward shifting of this tax. In
recent years, almost all of the distribution studies have utilized the total-
tax-bill technique.

To my knowledge, the earliest study that covered all of the taxes of
the central government was that prepared by the Colwyn Commission [3]
in the United Kingdom, in 1927, using the typical-family technique.
It thus extended the scope of the otherwise similar study by Lord
Samuel (released in 1919, for the years 1903–4, 1913–14, and 1918–
19), which had not dealt with income taxes.[4] In addition to its pioneering work, this tax-distribution study was notable for stimulating review
articles by Keynes [5] and Robertson,[6] the former commendatory, the
latter critical.

The earliest tax-distribution study of an entire tax system made in
the United States is apparently the one published in the Report of the
New York State Commission for the Revision of the Tax Laws, 1932,[7]
which used the typical-family method to distribute state and local taxes
(not federal taxes) imposed in New York State. The state taxes were on
motor fuel, operator's license (fee), motor vehicles (registration), in-

[3] Report of the Committee on National Debt and Taxation. Cmd. 2800. 1927.

[4] H. Samuel, "The Taxation of the Various Classes of the People," *Journal
of the Royal Statistical Society,* LXXXII, March, 1919, pp. 144–82. See also, for
post-Colwyn studies, D. C. Jones, "Pre-War and Post-War Taxation," *Journal of
the Royal Statistical Society,* Part IV, XC, 1927, pp. 685–718, and D. M. Sandral,
"The Burden of Taxation on the Various Classes of the Community," *Journal of
the Royal Statistical Society,* Part I, XCIV, 1931, pp. 83–94.

[5] J. M. Keynes, "The Colwyn Report on National Debt and Taxation,"
Economic Journal, June, 1927, pp. 198–212. Keynes' article reproduces in full the
Committee's detailed table of distribution of national-government taxes by income
levels, for each of five years, ranging from 1903–1904 to 1925–1926; and by tax:
all for a married taxpayer with three children under sixteen, *Ibid.,* pp. 200–201.

[6] Robertson was unhappy [correctly so] over the model of corporate behavior
devised by W. H. Coates, in which income tax could not "enter into price"; and
tested by Coates against data on profit margins. But whatever the faults of Coates'
procedure, he deserves credit for being the first [and also the last, apparently!] to
construct a model, however crude, in connection with his tax-distribution study,
and to attempt to test it. D. H. Robertson, "The Colwyn Committee, the Income
Tax and the Price Level," *Economic Journal* (Dec., 1927), pp. 566–81. Reprinted
in his *Economic Fragments.* London, King & Son, 1931.

[7] Legislative Document (1932) No. 77, State of New York, "Part Two, Report Submitted to the Commission by Robert Murray Haig," pp. 91–100.

surance, stock transfer, mortgage recording, personal income, estates, banks, corporation income (franchise), utility companies, and (local) real estate. This study's estimates of taxes paid directly or indirectly by a specified family (four families were specified) were decidedly impressionistic; but it did face up, if only briefly, to problems of allocation of taxes on long-lived assets (tax capitalization), on insurance contracts, on estates, on corporate income, on business real estate—as distinct from residential real estate—and on that portion of the property that could be labeled land.

The next detailed tax-distribution study,[8] and apparently the first in any country to include taxes of all levels of government, was that by Professor Mabel Newcomer in the Twentieth Century Fund research project of 1937.[9] The Newcomer study also broke new ground by computing a family's tax bill, direct and indirect, as a percentage of potential income rather than of recorded pretax income, and by comparing results under five series of assumptions about (a) shifting and incidence and (b) intrafamily changes in property ownership induced by tax provisions. Potential income is the income the family would have received in the absence of the tax system; for example, increased dividend income in the absence of a corporation income tax, and decreased income from land in the absence of an already capitalized land tax.[10] As did Coates,

[8] A brief updating and expansion of the New York State computations, this time using budget data for families from the United States Department of Labor, as found in "Depression Taxes and Economy through Reform of Local Government: Third Report of the New York State Commission for Revision of the Tax Laws" (Luther Gulick, Director of Research). Legislative Document No. 56 (1933), pp. 21–23. A detailed study of the distribution of property and income taxes was given by Harold Groves in his *Ability to Pay and the Tax System in Dane County*. Wisconsin, Bulletin of the University of Wisconsin, Bureau of Business and Economic Research, No. 2.

[9] Research Director, Carl Shoup; Associate Directors, Roy Blough and Mabel Newcomer, *Studies in Current Tax Problems*. New York, Twentieth Century Fund, 1937.

[10] With a given dollar capital to invest in land, the buyer gets less pretax income from his investment if there is no tax, since the price of land is correspondingly higher. Or, as Professor Newcomer put it, "In deducting the amount of [the annual payments for the] capitalized land tax [from actual income, to arrive at potential income], it has been assumed that the higher price that would have been paid [for an unchanged amount of land] if there had been no tax on land would have reduced the taxpayers' investments in securities, and therefore their incomes, by a corresponding amount." Mabel Newcomer, "Estimate of the Tax Burden on Different Income Classes," in Shoup, Blough and Newcomer, *op. cit.*, p. 31.

Newcomer limited her study to a one-size family: a married couple with two minor children. Computations were made for ten representative families with actual income ranging from five-hundred dollars to $1 million annually, distributed over six occupations, but assumed to be as much alike with respect to consumption patterns as was consistent with the differences in income and activity. Two geographic settings were employed, and the results compared: New York State (outside of New York City) and Illinois. The former state depended heavily upon the income tax; the latter, upon the general sales tax. As noted above, in each instance five alternative sets of assumptions were used regarding the shifting of certain taxes, and concerning the division of ownership of property between spouses (important for computing the family income-tax bill). Thus, for any one income level, ten alternative answers were obtained (two states, five sets of assumptions of the kind just noted).

In its wealth of detail regarding the assumptions made and the reasons for selecting them, the Newcomer study remains a useful source for anyone who is engaged in studies of tax distribution.[11]

[11] The findings of the Newcomer study were summarized in Carl Shoup, Roy Blough, and Mabel Newcomer, *Facing the Tax Problem*. New York, Twentieth Century Fund, 1937, Ch. 17. For details of the sets of assumptions, see Newcomer, *op. cit.*, p. 11. ". . . the smallest burden under any conditions is estimated to be 8 per cent of potential income, for one of the Illinois farm families, and the largest exceeds 100 per cent, in the extreme case of a corporation official where the family has an actual income of $1,000,000 but no steps are taken to distribute the income or property among members of the family in order to lessen income or death taxes [and where] . . . the family attempts to keep the property intact, on the death of the head of the family, through insurance sufficient to cover death taxes. . . . All the estimates indicate that the tax burden is regressive for those in income classes not subject to income and death taxes. This regressivity is largely due to the assumptions that the ratio of expenditures to income is greater for small incomes than for large incomes and that the rate of assessment [for real estate tax] is higher for small properties than for large properties. . . . Comparing the difference in estimated burdens under the different series of assumptions [concerning the shifting of taxes and pattern of ownership of property and income within the family], it is perhaps surprising to find that radical differences in assumptions result in comparatively small changes in [tax] burdens in most instances. . . ." Shoup, Blough, and Newcomer, *op. cit.*, pp. 231–32, 232–34, and 235, respectively. The median figure (of the five figures resulting from the five sets of assumptions) for total tax burden, federal, state, and local, as a percentage of the potential income, was, for New York: Farmers: $500, 15.0; $1,000, 11.4; $2,000, 9.8. Wage earners: $1,000, 17.6; $2,000, 16.4. Salaried worker: $5,000, 20.8. Merchant: $5,000, 24.5. Salaried worker: $20,000, 31.6. Corporation officials: $100,000, 44.3; $1,000,000, 84.5. For Illinois families, the respective percentages (medians) are: 12.7, 10.4, 9.2, 16.9, 15.9, 19.3, 40.7 (*sic*), 27.7, 39.9, and 81.0. *Ibid.*, Table 26, p. 232.

The next step, transition from the typical-family technique to the total-tax-bill technique, first appeared in published form [12] in an article by Robert R. Pettengill,[13] who blew up the Newcomer findings into a national aggregate set of figures, and in so doing, reached a tax revenue total close to the estimated actual total.

The second published study of this type took the actual total of tax revenue—federal, state, and local—and allocated it among income groups (*Who Pays the Taxes?* written under the supervision of Gerhard Colm, by Helen Tarasov [14]). The most striking difference from the findings of the Newcomer study concerned the lowest income group (lowest income level, in Newcomer). Colm-Tarasov found 21.9 per cent of the zero-to-$500 income group's average income of $346 going in taxes, against Newcomer's range of 11.2 per cent to 15.6 per cent for nine of her ten families with $500 income (the tenth showed 19.1 per cent). The difference in percentages is probably explained partly by the differences in income level. The remaining difference is explained partly by techniques of computation.[15]

In another thoughtful monograph in this area, John H. Adler [16] presented a United States federal-state-local tax distribution for 1946–47, together with a distribution of the benefits of government services

[12] Dr. Louis Shere had completed a more elaborate study of this type for the federal government in 1935, which was not published.

[13] "Division of the Tax Burden Among Income Groups in the United States in 1936," *American Economic Review,* XXX, 1940, pp. 60–71.

[14] Temporary National Economic Committee, Monograph No. 3, 1941 (*vii*, 55 pp.), Washington, D.C.

[15] For a critique written at that time, see the review of the Colm-Tarasov study by Carl Shoup, *Review of Economics and Statistics,* Feb., 1942, pp. 36–41. Tarasov later revised the study and updated it to 1941, without appreciable change in the findings: "Who Does Pay the Taxes?" Supplement IV to *Social Research,* 1942 (*xiii* + 49 pp.), Introduction by Jacob Marschak. Newcomer distributed to consumers only the nonland part of the business property tax, and distributed that part in the ratio that cash income bore to national income, instead of in the ratio that expenditures bore to the total of consumer expenditures. These two facts account for 3.5 percentage points of the difference. The absence of a sales tax in New York State (excluding New York City) explained another 2 percentage points for that part of the Newcomer study dealing with New York (but not, of course, for the part dealing with Illinois, where the difference was that much smaller to begin with, since Illinois did impose a sales tax). Most of the rest of the difference could not be explained, owing to a lack of published detail in the Colm-Tarasov study.

[16] "The Fiscal System, the Distribution of Income, and Public Welfare," Chapter VIII in Kenyon E. Poole, *Fiscal Policies and the American Economy.* New York, Prentice-Hall, 1951.

and transfer payments for that year. In addition, this work linked up with the Tarasov study for 1938–39. Adler's tax findings for 1946–47 did not differ materially from those of Tarasov. On the expenditures side, his distribution employed a number of allocators. Veterans' benefits were allocated equally among all consumer units below $5,000 ($2,000 for 1938–39); social security benefits and housing expenditures, equally to those below $4,000 ($2,000 in 1938–39); agricultural benefits, in proportion to income distribution among farmers; means-test expenditures (relief, medical), inversely to income below $4,000 ($2,500 in 1938–39); interest payments, on the basis of liquid asset holdings; police, fire, and other protection outlays, on the basis of real property holdings; educational expenditures, per capita; public works and road outlays, proportional to income; military, executive-office, and other miscellaneous expenditures, also proportional to income.[17]

Combining his tax and government service-and-payments allocations, Adler concluded that the fiscal system as a whole was progressive for both of those years. The interpretation was necessarily blurred by the fact that in 1938–39 the government sector operated at a substantial deficit, while in 1946–47 it showed a surplus, so that, in the earlier year, total benefits received exceeded taxes paid and, in the later year, fell short of taxes. Adler's discussion only partly resolved this troublesome conceptual issue. In any event, the lower-income groups either gained more, or lost less—in percentage terms—from the existence of a fiscal system than did the upper-income groups. But, of course, these methods of reckoning do not venture to suggest what the country would be like without any government at all, in which case the rich would probably be relatively better off than the poor, at least as long as they remained rich in a chaotic society.

To return to tax distributions, the most elaborate study of all appeared in the *National Tax Journal* for March, 1951 (pp. 1–53): "Distribution of Tax Payments by Income Groups: A Case Study for 1948," by R. A. Musgrave, J. J. Carroll, L. D. Cook, and L. Frane. This Musgrave study [as we shall call it] startled some of its readers by its extraordinary figure of 28.1 per cent of the income of those in the under-$1,000 class being taken in taxation (16.5 federal, 5.8 state, 5.8 local), compared with 24.3 per cent for the $1,000–under-$2,000 class, and 29.2 per cent for all income groups together.[18] The federal corporation income tax accounted for 7.3 points out of the 28.1, under Mus-

[17] *Ibid.*, pp. 384–87.
[18] *Ibid.*, Table 6, p. 26.

grave's "standard assumption" (Case A) that one-third of the tax was shifted forward to consumers, one-eighth backward to wage earners, with the rest burdening the shareholders.

Rufus S. Tucker, in an elaborate critique of Musgrave, concluded that the $0–$1,000 group paid only 18.7 per cent of their income in taxes, instead of 28.1 per cent.[19] Substantial comments on Musgrave appeared later, in an article by Gerhard Colm and Haskell Wald,[20] along with a Musgrave-Frane rejoinder to Dr. Tucker, a rebuttal by Tucker, and a concluding note by Musgrave and Frane.[21] Anyone who wants to become acquainted with the chief conceptual and computational pitfalls in this area will benefit from a study of this sheaf of excellent analyses. The chief reason for the differences in findings for the lowest income group turned out to be not so much the differing assumptions about tax shifting, but the alternative definitions of income classes by money income and by money plus imputed income (not including, however, imputed income from work in the home).

Meanwhile, in the United Kingdom, G. Findlay Shirras and L. Rostas had published in 1943 [22] a detailed tax-distribution study for 1937–38 and for the early war period; but they, as had their predecessors, omitted "rates" (local real estate taxes). Tibor Barna's monumental study for the year 1937,[23] published in 1945, not only included rates (distributed, as rates on dwellings, in proportion to expenditure on rent; and as rates on business, by type of business, thence to consumers by budget-study data), but also, for the first time,[24] a distribution of the benefits of government transfer payments and services. A few years later Allan M. Cartter published a similar study for postwar Britain.[25]

Several more tax-distribution studies and, less frequently, expenditure-distribution studies were made in the 1950's and 1960's; but they

[19] Rufus S. Tucker, "Distribution of Tax Burdens in 1948," *National Tax Journal* (Sept., 1951), pp. 269–85.

[20] *National Tax Journal* (March, 1952), pp. 1–14.

[21] *Ibid.,* pp. 15–35, pp. 36–38, and p. 39, respectively.

[22] *The Burden of British Taxation.* New York, Macmillan, 1943.

[23] *Redistribution of Incomes through the Fiscal System in 1937.* Oxford, Clarendon Press, 1945. For expenditure distribution, see pp. 76–84, pp. 195–213.

[24] Excepting the somewhat incidental reckoning made by Colin Clark, in *National Income and Outlay.* London, Macmillan, 1938 (cited by Adler, *op. cit.,* p. 365). In 1950, Hubert Brochier's *Finances Publiques et Redistribution des Revenus* (Paris, Armand-Colin), presented a tax-expenditure distribution for France.

[25] A. M. Cartter, *The Distribution of Income in Post-War Britain.* New Haven, Yale University Press, 1952.

will be cited only briefly here, for the essential issues had already been isolated in the formative period extending roughly from 1920 to 1950.[26] Tucker went on to distribute government benefits.[27] Musgrave made a study of 1954 data for the Joint Committee.[28] George A. Bishop utilized the Department of Commerce series on size distribution of family personal-income to distribute the 1958 tax bill.[29] Some studies of state tax-systems have distributed state and local taxes in those states.[30] The Council of Economic Advisers included in its Annual Report, dated January, 1969,[31] a chart distributing—among seven income groups— federal, and state-local taxes; and separately, transfer payments. The rates of tax computed as a percentage of income differ markedly from those of slightly earlier studies. The Council Report makes no reference to such studies. The difference arises chiefly, it appears, because income is here defined to exclude transfer payments. Those with income under $2,000 (defined in this fashion) are said to have received $16,622 million income in 1965, and, in addition, $21,025 million in transfer payments. Total taxes for 1965 allocated to this group of people were $7,296 million ($3.1 billion, federal; $4.1 billion, state and local). These

[26] Tax-distribution studies for countries other than the United States, in addition to those already noted, include: I. J. Goffman, *The Burden of Canadian Taxation.* Toronto, Canadian Tax Foundation, 1962, and "Incidence of Taxation in Canada," *Public Finance,* No. 1 (1964); F. D. Holzman, "The Burden of Soviet Taxation," *American Economic Review* (Sept., 1953); K. W. Roskamp, "The Distribution of Tax Burden in a Rapidly Growing Economy: West Germany in 1950," *National Tax Journal* (March, 1963); G. Zeitel. *Die Steuerlast in der Bundesrepublik Deutschland* (Tübingen, 1959); H. F. Lydall, "The Long-Term Trend in the Size Distribution of Income," *Journal of the Royal Statistical Society* (122, 1959), pp. 1–36; Merrett and Monk, "The Structure of U.K. Taxation, 1962–63," *Bulletin of the Oxford University Institute of Economics and Statistics* (Aug., 1966), and the Central Statistical Office's occasional articles on the effect of direct and indirect taxes and benefits on income distribution, published in the monthly journal *Economic Trends* (London); see, e.g., the August, 1966, issue.

[27] "The Distribution of Government Burdens and Benefits," *American Economic Review* (May, 1953), pp. 518–34.

[28] "The Incidence of the Tax Structure and Its Effects on Consumption"; "Federal Tax Policy for Economic Growth and Stability." Panelists' Papers, *Subcommittee on Tax Policy, Joint Committee on the Economic Report* (Nov. 9, 1955), pp. 96–113.

[29] "The Tax Burden by Income Class, 1958," *National Tax Journal* (March, 1961), pp. 41–58.

[30] See note 33 below.

[31] *Economic Report of the President* (Jan., 1969), together with *The Annual Report of the Council of Economic Advisers.* Superintendent of Documents, Washington, D.C., 1969, p. 161.

taxes, stated as a percentage of income defined to exclude the transfer payments, came to 43.9 per cent of income—a far higher figure than that shown by any of the earlier studies. For this group, taxes less transfer payments came to *minus* 82.6 per cent of income, defined as noted.[32] If these taxes were computed as a percentage of income including transfer payments, the 43.9 per cent figure would drop to 19.4 per cent.

Under the Council's method of computing taxes as a percentage of income, a family with no income—but receiving transfer payments—would be shown to be paying taxes equal to an indefinitely large percentage of its "income"; and this would be so, no matter how small the absolute amount of these taxes. The advantages of this method of presentation are at least arguable. In any event, one may hope that in future computations of this kind the Council will not state its quantitative findings so briefly, and almost casually; for here, with only one chart and no tables, conclusions are presented which are not only potentially explosive politically and socially, but which, at the same time, give the impression of being at variance with the long line of earlier quantitative studies.

The extent to which a particular taxing jurisdiction—a state in the United States, for instance, or a city in one of the states—might be exporting its tax bill to households and firms located elsewhere was largely, if not entirely, ignored in studies cited up to this point, as was also the amount of taxation that might be imported. These questions were faced in the late 1950's, and in the 1960's, in studies of the distribution of state tax systems, where the relative importance of the open-economy element induced analysis of tax exporting and tax importing.[33] The most

[32] The Council Report itself presents no tabular material or reference to sources. The data here are based on the 11 pages of mimeographed material that the Council sends to those of its readers who wish to obtain a description, upon request, of the "data from a variety of sources," on which the chart is based. This document is entitled "Background and Basic Assumptions of Tax-Transfer Chart Data (p. 161 of 1969 Annual Report)," by David J. Ott. Joseph A. Pechman, in his *The Rich, the Poor, and the Taxes They Pay, Public Interest,* No. 17 (Fall, 1969: reprint available from Brookings), presents, on p. 33, an abbreviation of Ott's Table 3, which is the basis for the chart in the Council's Report.

[33] See O. H. Brownlee, *Estimated Distribution of Minnesota Taxes and Public Expenditures.* Minneapolis, 1960; T. F. Hady, "The Incidence of the Personal Property Tax," *National Tax Journal* (Dec., 1962), pp. 368–84; Edwin W. Hanczaryk and James H. Thompson, *The Economic Impact of the State and Local Taxes in West Virginia.* Morgantown, West Va., West Virginia Bureau of Business Research, 1958; F. H. Jackson, *Tax Burden and the Hawaiian Tax System.* Honolulu, 1960; M. S. Kendrick and F. H. Jackson, *Economic Impact of Tax Reduc-*

comprehensive and detailed analysis of this aspect of the tax-distribution problem was that put forward by Charles E. McLure, Jr.[34] McLure examined the open economies of the states of the United States, and imputed "the shares of the various taxes falling upon each group to the states of residence of its members. . . . We assume certain effects of the taxes upon prices of products [given competitive conditions in an open economy] and factors (price effects), and then on the basis of the residency of those experiencing those price effects, allocate the taxes to residents and nonresidents of the taxing state." [35] He found that "For the nation as a whole $10.2 billion or 25 percent of all state and local taxes collected in 1962 were borne by non-residents of the taxing state, according to our short-run analysis. In the long-run, $8.3 billion or 20 percent were exported." [36]

McLure recognized the need to use differential incidence, employing as his other tax, a hypothetical tax—or rather, tax system—postulated to be borne entirely by residents of the taxing state. For this purpose, he selected a (hypothetical) income tax levied on a residence basis, on the assumption that residence mobility is not high.[37]

Some conjectures will now be offered here regarding fruitful paths for future research in tax distribution, and in distribution of government transfer payments and services.

First, it would be advisable to break down the lowest income group into two subgroups: those who are probably there to stay for some time; and those who, because of their age level, or because of temporary difficulties, may not be found there the following year—or, at least, not in the second or third year—students, temporarily unemployed skilled workers, small businessmen having a bad year, and (depending on the

---

tion. Honolulu, 1960; William E. Koenkner and Glenn W. Fisher, *Tax Equity in North Dakota.* University of North Dakota, 1960; Richard A. Musgrave and Darwin W. Daicoff, "Who Pays the Michigan Taxes?" in Michigan Study Staff Papers. Lansing, Michigan, 1958; University of Wisconsin, Tax Study Committee, *Wisconsin's State and Local Tax Burden.* Madison, Wisconsin, 1959.

[34] "An Analysis of Regional Tax Incidence, with Estimation of Interstate Incidence of State and Local Taxes." Princeton University, Doctoral Dissertation, 1966. University Microfilms, Ann Arbor, Michigan (*viii* + 376 pp.). See also his "Tax Exporting in the United States: Estimates for 1962," in *National Tax Journal* (March, 1967), pp. 49–77, and "Commodity Tax Incidence in Open Economies," *National Tax Journal* (June, 1964).

[35] "An Analysis of Regional Tax Incidence . . . ," p. 10. (See above.)

[36] *Ibid.,* p. 312.

[37] *Ibid.,* pp. 30–31.

questions the distribution is designed to answer) those with a life ex-
pectancy of only a year or so.

The U-shaped distribution curve, found in virtually every tax-
distribution study, came to be expected early in this research, since the
lowest-income group obviously contained some transients whose only
future direction was up (or out, for the very elderly), and who, meanwhile, would normally be outspending their low incomes. And it may
well be that the data for the next one or two higher-income classes are
similarly ambiguous. Far preferable, but more difficult to implement,
would be a study using a time period longer than a year.

Second, the imputed income of housewives should be entered along
with other imputed (and untaxed) income and expenditure. Even a
rough guess would be better than continuing to accede to the natural
desire of national-income estimators to avoid so conjectural a figure.[38]

Third, those who construct such tax-distribution tables (including
myself) should be more cautious, more limited, in their interpretations
of what the tables show. Taken literally, one such table, standing by
itself, purports to inform the reader by how much the aggregate disposable income of each income class would increase if all the taxes were
repealed, and nothing else were done. But, of course, something else
would have to be done: substitute taxes imposed, inflation financing
adopted, government itself abolished. It is somewhat as if we computed
the wages-bill cost of everything we consume, and showed that bill as a
"burden," varying by income class, depending on how consumption patterns of rich and poor differ in the mix of capital-intensive goods which
they consume, and in the proportion of income devoted to consumption.
No one such table by itself could be of much use.

Nonetheless, a single-tax distribution table can be a starting point
for a fruitful analysis. A change in the tax system can be postulated, and
by a priori reasoning (a macromodel, specified as best as may be from
a multitude of data from the past) some conjectures can be reached
concerning a consequent change in distribution of real disposable-
income, by income classes. Even here, caution is required. The aggregate pretax income falling in any one income class will almost surely not
be the same in the second table, owing to changes in remuneration,

[38] Something much better than a rough guess is in prospect, thanks to the
work under way at the National Bureau of Economic Research, by John W.
Kendrick, Nancy Ruggles and Richard Ruggles, Elizabeth Simpson Wehle, and
Harold Wolozin. (See National Bureau of Economic Research, *Annual Report*,
June, 1968, pp. 64–66; and June, 1969, p. 56.)

hours of work, supply of capital, and similar variables—changes induced
by the postulated alteration of the tax system. Moreover, many individuals (or households) will be in a different pretax income class under
the second tax system.

Still, the dangers of drastic errors of interpretation are probably
not so great as to invalidate broad conclusions drawn from such comparisons of two or more tax-distribution tables. (The same remarks
apply, of course, to tables that include distribution of transfer payments
and the value of free government services.) What must be resisted is the
simple kind of declaration, unaccompanied by any statement of alterna-
tives, that a single such table demonstrates that, say, 20 per cent of the
income of the lowest income-group is taken in taxes. The meaning and
significance of such a statement are obscure.

In sum, the studies of tax burden by income classes, and by geographic areas, are of great economic and social significance, and the long
history of their construction is an important chapter in quantitative
research in public finance. However, in my opinion, interpretation of the
results thus gained needs revision from that common in the past.[39] To

[39] See Carl S. Shoup, *Public Finance*. Chicago, Aldine, 1969, pp. 7–15. Professor Musgrave offered a penetrating analysis of this issue in his 1951 article:
"The reader may wonder why, after having defined the concept of burden in
section 2 in terms of *absolute* money burden, we conducted the discussion in section 3 in terms of changes in the distribution of the money burden which result
when one tax system is substituted for another. Would it not have been simpler to
compare income net of tax under the given tax structure with income net of tax
in the absence of taxes and thus determine the absolute burden distribution of
the given tax structure? Unfortunately, this cannot be done, for the simple reason
that taxes are the counterpart of public expenditures. . . . In a situation where,
to begin with, we have public expenditures as well as taxes, we cannot 'think the
existing taxes away'—to borrow Wicksell's terms—without either (a) thinking
public expenditures away as well, or (b) substituting some alternative means of
finance. . . . In tax determination, the distribution of the money burden is of
primary importance. But, if we wish to study the incidence of taxation as such, it
must be recognized that this incidence cannot be thought of in absolute terms; an
alternative means of finance must be substituted when the prevailing taxes are
'thought away,' and this means that the result will necessarily be in differential
terms." R. A. Musgrave, J. J. Carroll, L. D. Cook and L. Frane, *loc. cit.*, pp. 6–8.
See also the excellent analysis by Alan R. Prest, "The Budget and Interpersonal
Distribution," in *Public Finance*, XXIII, 1968 (No. 1–2), pp. 80–98, and "Comment" by Karl W. Roskamp, pp. 99–105.
In Norway, the Central Bureau of Statistics issued on Aug. 19, 1965, a report entitled *Statistical Tax Incidence Investigation, 1960*, cast entirely in terms of
differential tax incidence. The hypothetical tax used as a basis for comparison
with the existing system of Norwegian direct taxes, indirect taxes, price subsidies,

accomplish this will require considerable self-restraint. It implies, for example, as the section below makes clear, that no broad-based tax can be said to have an incidence (as distinguished from its impact) of its own; it has only a differential incidence relative to some other public-finance measure.

The differential approach is taken naturally in those studies that appraise the structure of one particular tax and ask how some specified change in that structure—a change that would leave unaltered the yield of that tax—would affect the distribution of tax liability by income class, or by some other grouping. Or, short of this, they compute the revenue loss or gain to come from a certain structural change, and at least imply which of the income groups could not reasonably be called upon to make good the gap or be allowed to participate in the surplus, in view of the purpose behind the structural change.[40]

B. Shifting and Incidence of Taxes

In contrast to the quantitative work on tax and expenditure distribution, that on shifting and incidence has but recently entered its most

and social security contributions was a simple proportional income tax. "The differential tax shows how much worse (if the differential tax is negative: better) individual household groups were situated in 1960 as compared to how they would have been situated if the hypothetical tax system had been enforced. The comparison thus gives us a relative tax incidence." ("English summary," p. 83.) It was assumed that "the price a household pays for a consumer good is changed by an amount that equals the change in indirect taxes (less price subsidies) per unit" and that "the disposable income of the household would have been changed by an amount that equals the change in direct taxes (less transfers to the household from the government)" (p. 84). Further changes that might be expected from "various repercussions that a change in tax system will bring upon the economy through changes in the behaviour of individual households and firms" could not be taken into account in the absence of a comprehensive economic model. This report was the work of Mr. Arne Øien, who received aid and advice primarily from Professors Cary Brown and Leif Johansen, and from Per Sevaldson. From my point of view, this is precisely the kind of approach that should be used in tax distribution studies; it is to be hoped that this Norwegian study will serve as a model for future work in this field, though the particular hypothetical tax or tax system to be used as a base for comparison will, of course, vary with the circumstances.

[40] So many empirical studies of this type have been published that it would be difficult to attempt to record them here, but a notable recent example consists of the sections relevant to this point in Lawrence H. Seltzer, *The Personal Exemptions in the Income Tax*. National Bureau of Economic Research. New York, Columbia University Press, 1968.

interesting and puzzling stage, which, in this case, is the attempt to measure the degree of shifting, if any, of broad-based taxes—notably, the corporate income tax—by econometric analysis. Earlier quantitative studies had been concerned with narrowly based excises,[41] which can be usefully studied in a simple partial-equilibrium framework by observation of immediate changes in prices.[42] To be sure, there had been at least two attempts to ascertain the incidence of broad-based taxes, but neither one had employed sophisticated techniques. One was the study—flawed in its reasoning but imaginatively mounted—by Coates for the Colwyn Commission in 1927.[43] The other was the analysis of the incidence of the processing taxes of the 1930's in the United States, where an unexpected Supreme Court nullification of the taxes on January 6, 1936, had produced a clean break in a time series of prices and processing-cost margins, and so enabled a post hoc approach to achieve an apparently high degree of reliability.[44] These taxes had been imposed on the first domestic processing of wheat, cotton, hogs, and six other "basic agricultural commodities," under the Agricultural Adjustment Act of May 12, 1933; the actual introduction of the several taxes occurred in 1933, 1934, or 1935. The taxes were obviously intended to be shifted by the processors.[45]

Following nullification of the taxes, Congress included in the Revenue Act of 1936 a provision that processing taxes paid by the processors could be reclaimed by them, as refunds, only upon proof that they had failed to shift the tax. Certain firms that had benefited by others' shifting, without themselves having paid the tax, were made subject to an "unjust enrichment tax." In reaching decisions on cases brought before them, the United States courts were aided by the study cited in footnote

[41] See Oswald Brownlee and George L. Perry, "The Effects of the 1965 Federal Excise Tax Reductions on Prices," *National Tax Journal* (Sept., 1967); John F. Due, "The Effect of the 1954 Reduction of Federal Excise Taxes upon the List Prices of Electrical Appliances: a Case Study," *National Tax Journal* (Sept., 1954); Harry L. Johnson, "Tax Pyramiding and the Manufacturer's Excise Tax Reduction of 1954," *National Tax Journal* (Sept., 1964). See also note 50 below.

[42] Carl S. Shoup, *Public Finance*, pp. 9–10.

[43] Appendices to the *Report of the Commission on National Debt and Taxation*, pp. 65–113. (See notes 3, 5, and 6 in Section II-A above.)

[44] Bureau of Internal Revenue, United States Treasury Dept., *An Analysis of the Effects of the Processing Taxes Levied under the Agricultural Adjustment Act*. Washington, 1937. The study was made by the Bureau of Agricultural Economics of the United States Department of Agriculture.

[45] See Wirth F. Ferger, "The Measurement of Tax Shifting: Economics and the Law," *Quarterly Journal of Economics* (May, 1940), p. 431.

44. The findings of that study are too complex to be summarized adequately here, but in general, they indicated that the processors had indeed shifted the taxes. For example, upon initiation of the processing tax on wheat, the spread between the weekly price of wheat per bushel in Minneapolis and the value of the milled products obtained from a bushel of wheat (which had fluctuated only moderately in the preceding two years) rose at once so that the margin, after allowing for the tax, remained unchanged. When the tax was removed, in January 1936, the margin immediately declined by the full amount of the tax.[46] These margin changes did not, of course, show whether the taxes were shifted forward or backward.[47]

Other studies based on time series (made at various times and places) that were designed primarily to obtain information on aspects other than incidence, included some findings on apparent, very short-run incidence.[48, 49]

The studies referred to in note 41 above found that reductions or repeal of federal excise taxes in 1954, and in 1965, were promptly followed by reductions in suggested or actual retail prices of the commodities or services affected, commonly by an amount roughly equivalent to the tax reduction with a loading for tax pyramiding; i.e., applying a percentage markup to sales price including tax. But there were enough departures from this outcome to render impracticable here a brief summary of the results observed.[50]

[46] Wirth F. Ferger, "Windfall Tax and Processing Tax Refund Provisions of the 1936 Revenue Act," *American Economic Review* (1937), p. 54.

[47] Other types of studies had to be made to attack this problem; they indicated that most of the wheat and cotton processing taxes had been shifted forward, while a large part of the hog tax had been shifted backward. Ferger, *op. cit.,* p. 56, and sources there cited, e.g., Geoffrey Shepherd, "Incidence of the Processing Tax on Hogs," *Journal of Farm Economics* (May, 1935).

[48] See Robert Murray Haig and Carl Shoup, with the assistance of Reavis Cox, Louis Shere, and Edwin H. Spengler, *The Sales Tax in the American States.* New York, Columbia University Press, 1934, pp. 64–80, and Index, "Shifting."

[49] For much earlier studies, see references to Mildschuh (rentals tax in Prague); Laspeyres and Schott (milling and slaughtering taxes in Prussia); and Hellwig (Hessian octrois on flour and bread) in Otto von Mering, *The Shifting and Incidence of Taxation.* Philadelphia, Blakiston, 1942, pp. 7–8; and Horst Claus Recktenwald, *Steuerüberwälzungslehre.* Berlin, Duncker & Humblot, 1966, p. 70.

[50] See especially the findings of F. O. Woodward and Harvey Seigelman, "Effects of the 1965 Federal Excise Tax Reduction Upon the Prices of Automotive Replacement Parts—A Case Study in Tax Shifting and Pyramiding," *National Tax Journal* (Sept., 1967), that seemed to indicate that those auto parts, accessories, etc., for which the demand was presumably the most *elastic* showed the greatest decline in price, relative to the tax reduction. *Ibid.,* p. 256.

The first attempts to ascertain the incidence of the corporation income tax in the United States by appeal to time series were based on the curious fact that from the 1920's to the mid-1950's post-tax corporate profits in industry and trade changed very little if expressed as a return on book value of net worth, but declined appreciably as a percentage of sales, while the rate of the corporation income tax was increasing from 12.5 per cent to 52 per cent. In two articles written independently, John Clendenin,[51] and Eugene M. Lerner and Eldon S. Hendriksen,[52] concluded that these data indicated a shifting of the increases in the corporation income tax—probably forward, for the most part. Plausible nontax developments during that period (e.g., faster turnover of inventories) were adduced to explain the drop in profit as a percentage of sales. On the other hand, Edward T. Thompson and Charles E. Silberman [53] interpreted these data to mean that the increases in that tax had not been shifted. On the whole, the Clendenin-Lerner-Hendriksen conclusion seems more acceptable than that of Thompson and Silberman.[54] But the evidence is rather slender.

A new approach was developed with the appearance of the "empirical study of [the corporation income tax's] . . . short-run effect upon the rate of return," by Marian Krzyzaniak and Richard A. Musgrave.[55] The K-M Model "observes effects coming about within a year," [56] or "within a short period, i.e., a few years," [57] a period during which "fixed capital adjustments are hardly possible," [58] or "the effects of changes in capital stock in the corporate sector enter to a very limited degree only." [59] The study is limited to manufacturing corporations.[60]

Structural equations (definitional and behavioral) are given for production, aggregate demand, consumption, investment, labor supply,

[51] "Effect of Corporate Income Taxes on Corporate Earnings," *Taxes, The Tax Magazine* (June, 1956).

[52] "Federal Taxes on Corporate Income and the Rate of Return on Investment in Manufacturing," *National Tax Journal* (Sept., 1956).

[53] "Can Anything Be Done about Corporate Taxes?" *Fortune* (May, 1955).

[54] See the critique of these studies by Carl S. Shoup in "Some Problems in the Incidence of the Corporation Income Tax," *American Economic Review* (May, 1960), pp. 463–67.

[55] *The Shifting of the Corporation Income Tax.* Baltimore, Johns Hopkins Press, 1963. (The phrase quoted is the subtitle.)

[56] *Ibid.,* p. 2.

[57] *Ibid.,* pp. 4–5.

[58] *Ibid.,* p. 2.

[59] *Ibid.,* p. 5.

[60] *Ibid.,* p. 23.

labor demand, prices, rate of return, and the tax function itself; but aside from the last of these, no functional forms are given. (A few lagged variables are supplied.) The tax function in its "Model A" form, to which most attention is given, is $Y_g - Y' = \dfrac{aT}{K}$; that is, the before-tax rate of return on capital under the tax, minus the rate of return on capital in absence of the tax, equals a certain proportion: the ratio of the firm's tax bill to its capital stock.

No behavioral equation is supplied with respect to the business firm's attitude toward profits.

Throughout, K-M evince awareness of the point made in Section II-A above; namely, that an increase in the corporation income tax rate must make something else change: government expenditures increase, or some other tax is reduced, or government debt is retired, or the government's cash balance increases. K-M imply that the first of these is the most likely, or the most important, and accordingly point out that they are left with "a result which may come closer to that of budget effects than that of absolute corporation-tax effects." [61] This qualification is repeated several times: "the tax coefficient [degree of shifting, which in this case came to 134 per cent, with a 95 per cent confidence limit giving an interval from 111 per cent to 157 per cent] [62] is exaggerated by a G [government expenditure] effect which cannot be separated out. . . . That is to say, our measure is not only one of tax incidence, but is contaminated by influences of budget incidence." [63] When an adjustment for inflation has lowered the estimated degree of shifting to about 100 per cent, "this result still tends to overstate the degree of tax shifting because [government] expenditure effects are present. Thus, it appears that pure tax shifting will be below 100 per cent." [64] When profit is expressed as a share in value added, and only 40 per cent shifting is thereupon found, one reason may be that "the government expenditure effect which is not neutralized in our measure of rate-of-return shifting tends to be self-neutralizing in the share measure." [65]

Finally, the "stark outline of the major policy conclusions which

[61] *Ibid.*, pp. 6–7. ". . . it would hardly be possible to construct a model measuring 'differential' effects. The best we can do is to aim at 'absolute' effects, but even this proves difficult."

[62] *Ibid.*, p. 46.

[63] *Ibid.*, p. 47.

[64] *Ibid.*, p. 49.

[65] *Ibid.*, p. 65.

follow if the hypothesis of 100 per cent short-run shifting is accepted," a hypothesis "supported by our result for the all-manufacturing case, corrected for inflation," must evidently be viewed in light of the fact that "several reasons—especially failure to separate government expenditure effects—suggest that this result overstates the degree of short-run shifting." [66]

Yet despite these disclaimers, the title and the tone of the book suggest that what was discovered was indeed the degree of shifting of the corporation income tax. Reception of the findings might have been facilitated if the study had been entitled "The Effect on After-Tax Profits of Manufacturing Corporations Exerted by Changes in the Corporate Income Tax Rate and Associated Changes in Government Expenditures and Probably Other Government Variables," but the publisher might well have demurred.

R. J. Gordon's critique, interestingly enough, does not touch directly on this "expenditure contamination" aspect of the K-M findings, and his comments on the results under his own technique do not mention this point, save in a brief footnote that seems almost an afterthought.[67] Perhaps he decided that there was little need to make this point, since even without it, he arrives at a finding of zero shifting, either for a rate-of-return concept of profits or an income-share concept.

In contrast to K-M, Gordon derives his independent variables from "a model of the probable profit performance of firms that practice mark-up pricing behavior." [68] The finding that "the parameter of tax shifting is not significantly different from zero" [69] is reached when using the K-M time span, but employing a different method of estimation and—much more important according to Gordon—a different specification (different model). When the time period is extended to 1925–41 plus 1946–62, the results are strikingly similar. It might even be argued

---

[66] *Ibid.*, p. 66.

[67] "To test the effect of the corporation income tax on profit rates, we must be able to estimate the level of profit rates in the absence of the tax. Obviously we must assume that without a corporation income tax government revenues are maintained by some other kind of tax. Otherwise a diminution of government revenues would result in a change either in government spending or in the surplus-deficit position and thus in all the economic magnitudes which determine profits." Robert J. Gordon, "The Incidence of the Corporation Income Tax in U.S. Manufacturing, 1925–62," *American Economic Review* (Sept., 1967), p. 735, note 6.

[68] *Ibid.*, p. 733.

[69] *Ibid.*, p. 745.

that what Gordon has found, in the terminology of K-M, is an appreciable but unknown amount of negative shifting of the corporation income tax if his findings are "contaminated" by the government-expenditure effect as much as theirs are.

As with Gordon's analysis, that by John G. Cragg, Arnold C. Harberger, and Peter Mieszkowski [70] attacks the K-M findings on grounds other than the "contamination" factor. Adding the employment rate and a dummy variable to the K-M Model to capture the influence of cyclical and wartime phenomena, C-H-M obtain regression equations implying that corporations recouped only about half the increases in corporation income tax. Assuming that in the unincorporated sector, which competes with the incorporated sector for capital, the profit rate had to fall by about the same degree (here, by about one half of the tax) by which the corporate sector failed to recoup increases in the tax on it; and noting that about as much capital is employed in the one sector as in the other in total, C-H-M conclude that their variant of the K-M Model implies that total capital, incorporated and unincorporated, bore at least about 100 per cent of the increases in the corporation income tax: "at least" because their estimating procedure is admittedly biased in two ways that tend to overestimate the proportion of the tax that is shifted. [71] But C-H-M are unwilling to accept even their version of the K-M Model, in view of the inherent risks in the use of time series for this kind of study. [72, 73]

[70] "Empirical Evidence on the Incidence of the Corporation Income Tax," *Journal of Political Economy* (Dec., 1967).

[71] *Ibid.*, p. 820.

[72] *Ibid.*, p. 821. See also the C-H-M Rejoinder to the K-M Response on Corporation Tax Shifting, *Journal of Political Economy* (July-Aug., 1970), p. 774: "the pitfalls associated with estimating corporation tax incidence from time-series data, in K-M fashion, are too numerous and serious for the results to be trustworthy."

[73] Space limitations prevent recapitulation here of the lengthy and cogent critiques of the K-M analysis given by Richard Goode, "Rate of Return, Income Shares, and Corporate Tax Incidence," and Richard E. Slitor, "Corporate Tax Incidence: Economic Adjustments to Differentials under a Two-Tier Tax Structure," in Marian Krzyzaniak, ed., *Effects of Corporation Income Tax*. Detroit, Wayne State University Press, 1966; the study by R. W. Kilpatrick, "The Short-Run Forward Shifting of the Corporation Income Tax," *Yale Economic Essays* (Fall, 1965); the findings reached by Challis Hall, "Direct Shifting of the Corporation Income Tax in Manufacturing," *American Economic Review* (May, 1964), pp. 258–71; and the application of the K-M Model to another country by Karl W.

Future empirical research at the partial-equilibrium level, covering changes in excise-tax rates, might well continue along the lines developed by Due, Brownlee, and others. Readiness is important, enabling the researcher to seize the occasion when it arises. To this end, the National Bureau, or some other research body, might stockpile techniques and avenues of information so that a study could be mounted quickly when a tax reduction or a tax increase appeared imminent. For example, some information might be gathered on the industry structure, and pricing policies, of the cigarette industry (including the wholesalers and retailers of cigarettes) so that we might know in advance something about what to expect, and where to go to observe the price changes when a tax on cigarettes is altered.

As to the broad-based taxes, however, a prescription is much more difficult. A number of major questions have to be answered before further research is actually started. Is the time-series technique pioneered in this field by Krzyzaniak and Musgrave as risky as Cragg, Harberger, and Mieszkowski fear? If it is not, just how are the shifting coefficients to be interpreted (the contamination problem)? Does the divergence of findings, e.g., K-M versus Gordon, indicate an inherent complexity that cannot be mastered, or does it simply mean that we learn by doing? Can a general-equilibrium model of the kind outlined by Bossons and Shoup [74] ascertain the effects of the substitution of one tax for another? Is there an implied negative answer to this question in Musgrave's remark that it is hardly possible to construct a model measuring differential effects? [75]

I have no firm answers to these questions. Perhaps the prescription is: set enough research teams on the problem with enough different approaches to enable us to learn much more about what we face. The one certain thing seems to be that we are many years, perhaps several decades, away from firm knowledge in this field, and that aside from time and money, which are always helpful, we shall need large amounts of daring laced with modesty.

Roskamp, "The Shifting of Taxes on Business Income: The Case of the West German Corporations," *National Tax Journal* (Sept., 1965), pp. 247–57.

[74] John Bossons and Carl S. Shoup, "Analyzing the Effects of Large-Scale Changes in Fiscal Structure: A Proposed Systems Approach," in National Bureau of Economic Research, *New Challenges for Economic Research*, Forty-Ninth Annual Report (Oct., 1969), pp. 11–26.

[75] See note 61 above.

C. Effects of Taxes on Investment and Other Business Behavior

(1) Effects on Investment.   Until fairly recently, there was little in the way of empirical studies of the effects of tax measures on investment—in the national-income sense of investment. The Colwyn Committee's efforts to discern the incidence of the income tax on profits (referred to in note 6 above) carried implications for this issue. Studies of how tax changes affected portfolio investment also supplied indirect evidence on bricks-and-mortar investment, notably Lawrence H. Seltzer's monumental work, under National Bureau auspices, on capital gains and losses under the United States federal income-tax.[76] In succeeding years, the National Bureau led the way in gathering and analyzing data on the impact of the federal income-tax system on dividends and profits in general, while abstaining from conjecture as to the effects of these tax rates on investment decisions. Holland contributed two monographs on the federal income-tax burden on stockholders,[77] containing further facts relevant to the investment issue but not directly attacking the problem of ascertaining what the consequences might be. Lent's study of the ownership of tax-exempt securities for the period 1919–1953 [78] filled in another background segment by discovering that the concentration of ownership of such securities among the high-income individuals was somewhat less than might have been expected on pecuniary grounds. Kahn's detailed analysis of income and income-tax liabilities of unincorporated concerns, including the professions, covered a part of the business field that had been rather neglected.[79]

In the past few years, research has been more directly oriented to the question, Is business investment affected by the kinds of tax change the western world has experienced over the past several decades? and, if so, in what directions and in what approximate magnitudes? Three approaches have been utilized.

[76] *The Nature and Tax Treatment of Capital Gains and Losses* (with the assistance of Selma F. Goldsmith and M. Slade Kendrick). New York, National Bureau of Economic Research, 1951.

[77] Daniel M. Holland, *The Income-Tax Burden on Stockholders,* Princeton University Press, 1958; and *Dividends under the Income Tax,* Princeton University Press, 1962.

[78] George E. Lent, *The Ownership of Tax-Exempt Securities, 1913–1953,* Occasional Paper 47. New York, National Bureau of Economic Research, 1955.

[79] C. Harry Kahn, *Business and Professional Income under the Personal Income Tax.* A Study by the National Bureau of Economic Research. Princeton University Press, 1964.

One is to ascertain the extent to which business firms do take advantage of accelerated depreciation allowances and similar tax inducements to invest. If, because of ignorance or overriding nontax considerations, firms make little use of these incentives, the analysis can stop there until more is learned about the theory of the firm. Ture's findings, covering both corporations and unincorporated enterprises in the United States with respect to the accelerated depreciation introduced in 1954, show that we cannot stop there, since the data for the first six or seven years of experience with these new provisions indicate that "a large proportion of the depreciable facilities acquired by corporations since 1953 and still on hand in 1959 was in accelerated method accounts." [80] Ture goes on to a conjecture—based on a range of assumed elasticities of the demand and supply functions for these facilities,[81]—that outlays were from $1.3 billion to $5.7 billion more in 1959 than they would have been in the absence of the 1954 innovation.[82] This finding rests, of course, on far less secure ground than do those simply describing the extent to which accelerated depreciation was, in fact, used.

For me, at least, the importance of the distinction between a firm's willingness to accept the chance to reduce taxes by using accelerated depreciation and the degree to which it allows such tax-saving to influence its investment decisions was enhanced by the appalling findings of Stanback,[83] obtained in interviews with executives of twenty-five textile firms concerning practice, in that industry, in face of inducements to investment created by the more generous depreciation provisions and the introduction of the investment-tax credit in 1962. I use the word *appalling,* because only 36 per cent of the firms interviewed used investment computation formulas that made explicit any part of the tax-savings of liberalized depreciation. More than half of this group, to be sure, was composed of large firms. Nonetheless, it must have a sobering effect on the tax theorist to be informed that not only did the other 64 per cent of the firms use rules for investment that took no account of this tax saving, but also that "there was little evidence that, at time of interview, these firms were recognizing [even] informally . . . that

[80] Norman B. Ture, *Accelerated Depreciation in the United States, 1954–60.* National Bureau of Economic Research. New York, Columbia University Press, 1967, p. 97.

[81] *Ibid.,* p. 95.

[82] *Ibid.,* p. 97.

[83] Thomas M. Stanback, Jr., *Tax Changes and Modernization in the Textile Industry.* National Bureau of Economic Research. New York, Columbia University Press, 1969.

liberalized depreciation resulted in reduction in the after-tax pay-back period, or in an increase in the effective rate of return." [84, 85]

A second approach is the comparative one, in which public finance analysts accept assignments to appraise the effects of recent tax policies on investment in their respective countries, then meet to refine their conclusions, or conjectures, by conference discussion. The NBER and The Brookings Institution held such a conference in 1963.[86] The descriptions of the various tax techniques used to stimulate growth expanded the range of the observers' propensity for a priori model-building. Many misconceptions as to what had been attempted elsewhere were removed. The conference paid substantial intellectual dividends. But, as E. Gordon Keith remarked in his Introduction and Summary, it became evident that "much too little is known about the actual effects of specific tax measures on the savings and investment decisions of individuals and corporations." None of the conferees who formed opinions on the tax effects were "able to offer much empirical support for their positions." [87]

A third approach is econometric, employing either time series or cross-sectional data, observing how the rate of investment differs, and attempting to isolate the degree to which these differences are due to tax changes. This approach is well illustrated in the volume shortly to be published by The Brookings Institution, *Tax Incentives and Capital Spending*,[88] containing four papers designed "to develop models of fixed

[84] *Ibid.*, p. 103. Professor Stanback himself does not employ language as forceful as mine in appraising the investment attitudes he discovered, but the closing paragraphs on his p. 105 should be required reading for all tax economists. I am indebted to David Stout for the following observation: "Similarly disturbing findings emerged from the questioning of Directors of fourteen U.K. corporations as reported by the Richardson Committee on Turnover Taxation in 1964. However, by 1969, on a much wider survey of industrial responses to changes in the effective rate of corporate taxation there was a good deal more evidence of tax-consciousness in pricing and investment decisions. See National Economic Development Office, *Value Added Tax*, Chapter 6. A comprehensive postal questionnaire and case-study interview inquiry into the effects of accelerated depreciation and cash grants for investment by the U.K. Ministry of Technology is nearing completion."

[85] Challis Hall's interview survey of the effects of changes in the corporate income tax on investment decisions over a wide spectrum of industry was halted by his untimely death.

[86] National Bureau of Economic Research and The Brookings Institution, *Foreign Tax Policies and Economic Growth*. New York, Columbia University Press, 1966.

[87] *Ibid.*, p. 37.

[88] My comments on, and quotations from, this volume are based on a copy of the page proof kindly supplied by The Brookings Institution in August, 1970.

investment behavior of United States business firms and to evaluate the impact on capital spending of federal tax incentives enacted since the end of the Second World War." [89] These papers were the subject of a conference at which Discussion Papers were presented by Franklin M. Fisher and Arnold C. Harberger.[90]

This is a very illuminating volume if only because it makes so evident the enormous difficulty of isolating the quantitative effects of a tax measure. Although the four papers "were prepared by competent scholars" [91]—indeed, Fisher remarks, the four analyses "are all marked by high quality," each one applying "sophisticated econometric tools . . . in a professional and convincing manner" [92]—and although each paper "had the objective of measuring the same phenomena," yet, in the event, "each obtained a significantly different answer." [93]

While Fromm remarks that "this is no cause for despair," [94] and expresses the hope that "improvements in theory and refinements in the data will lead to more definitive conclusions," [95] Harberger seems less optimistic: "The basic trouble is that, in much of their work, economists are destined to deal with a limited body of data." [96] Fisher, perhaps, falls in between: "I cannot pretend to resolve these contradictions here. But I can hope to promote their resolution" [97] by a systematic analysis of the four treatments. In contrast to Fromm and Harberger, Fisher is willing to state a preference: "I am slightly more disposed to accept the results of [Charles W.] Bischoff [98] and of [Lawrence R.] Klein and [Paul] Taubman [99] than those of [Robert M.] Coen [100] and of [Robert E.] Hall and [Dale W.] Jorgenson." [101, 102]

We must recall that, even if these papers had reached agreement,

[89] Gary Fromm, ed., *op. cit.*, Ch. I, Introduction, p. 1.

[90] *Ibid.*, Chs. VI and VII, respectively.

[91] Fromm, *op. cit.*, p. 1.

[92] *Ibid.*, p. 243.

[93] Fromm, *op. cit.*, p. 1. The differences in the answers are themselves too complex to be summarized readily here.

[94] *Ibid.*, p. 1.

[95] *Idem.*

[96] *Ibid.*, p. 257.

[97] *Ibid.*, p. 243.

[98] "The Effect of Alternative Lag Distributions," *op. cit.*, Ch. III.

[99] "Estimating Effects within a Complete Econometric Model," *op. cit.*, Ch. V.

[100] "The Effect of Cash Flow on the Speed of Adjustment," *op. cit.*, Ch. IV.

[101] Application of the Theory of Optimum Capital Accumulation," *op. cit.*, Ch. II.

[102] Fromm, *op. cit.*, p. 255.

they would have told us nothing about the effect of the tax changes on investment in total. This was not their task. They were concerned only with the effects of federal income tax changes that introduced accelerated depreciation in 1954; new shorter lifetimes for depreciating investment, and the investment credit, in 1962; the decrease in tax rates, particularly the corporate profits tax rate, in 1964; and suspension of the investment credit for a part of 1966–67. None of these tax measures applied to all private investment, and the investment credit was restricted to equipment of more than a certain expected life.

Harberger remarks that "most proponents of this [tax relief] legislation" probably thought that it "would increase investment in the U.S. economy in relation to some measure . . . such as gross national product. . . ."[103] Yet, in fact, investment as a percentage of GNP was slightly less from 1962 through the first half of 1967 than from 1955 through 1961. "The answer lies largely in the truism that investment must equal savings for the economy as a whole," while "the tax measures under consideration . . . provided no clear incentive to savings."[104]

Rather, these measures were, in part, the cause of a change in the composition of investment, away from residential construction to other private domestic nonresidential investment, principally plant and equipment spending.[105]

Two other points that Harberger makes are particularly telling, especially since they lie quite apart from most of the technical disagreements over methods of approach that occupy the authors of the four papers.

First, it seems odd that three of the papers should be, apparently, so vulnerable to the charge of having ignored the simple but basic point that if the corporation income tax rate alone is raised, there will be some diversion of capital into the unincorporated sector, with a consequent tendency for the pretax rate of return on capital to rise in the former sector, and to fall in the latter.[106]

Harberger's second point is more serious:

"Hall and Jorgenson, Bischoff and Coen simply bypass all general equilibrium considerations and concentrate on attempting to measure the direct price effect of the incentives. They therefore cannot

[103] *Ibid.*, p. 263.
[104] *Idem.*
[105] *Ibid.*, pp. 263–64.
[106] This criticism applies to the papers by Hall-Jorgenson, Bischoff, and Coen. *Ibid.*, pp. 260–61, 262.

purport to say anything about the total effect. The total effect must be less than the direct effect where alternative monetary policy would have kept the time path of income the same; it must be greater than the direct effect where alternative monetary policy would have kept the time path of interest rates the same; and it can be either greater or less than the direct effect in the case where the alternative policy would have maintained the same time path of the money supply—all this in the context of the simple models outlined [by Harberger] above, and referring only to covered [i.e., directly affected by the tax measure] investment." [107]

When one considers that, along with the points made in the preceding five paragraphs, there are the formidable technical issues of choice of econometric techniques (discussed at some length in all of the papers, and in the two Discussions), optimism does not come easily. But we must remind ourselves that the difficulty is great only because the aim is so high: no less than to extract quantitative answers, on which all will agree (or almost agree), as to the effects on certain types of investment decisions of tax changes made over a period of time in which so many other forces were operating on these same decisions. Perhaps we shall be, for some time yet, limited to the general kind of conclusions reached by Harberger, largely on a priori reasoning, with fairly simple models:

"In sum, therefore, the quality of the work presented here is very high, but the analyses leave unfinished and unclear the picture of the quantitative effects of the tax incentives that have been examined. I remain prone to the same rough judgment about these incentives that I have held for several years: that they played an important role in permitting us to come reasonably close to full employment in the presence of a strong balance-of-payments constraint; that they accomplished this by creating a situation in which the interest rate level consistent with full employment was significantly higher than it otherwise would be; that, viewed against alternative ways of achieving full employment, these tax stimuli produced a massive shift of investment from the noncovered sector (principally residential housing) to the covered sector, without much change in total investment; and that, viewed against the alternative of maintaining the same interest-rate or balance-of-pay-

107 *Ibid.,* pp. 267–68.

ments posture that obtained, the incentives probably account for a significant increase in total investment and in income." [108]

As the reader of the present monograph has probably gathered by now, I am particularly attracted by Harberger's insistence on specifying the alternative with which the existing situation is to be compared if some sort of general-equilibrium answer is to be implied in the findings.

(2) Effects on Other Business Behavior.   Effects of taxation on business behavior other than investment spending—and other than changes in prices and factor payments covered under the discussion of incidence—are so numerous as to defy any attempt at listing them. This need not be tried here, anyway, since few of these effects have been the subject of quantitative study. The present section is limited to some brief remarks on the effects on financial structure and on methods of wage, or salary, payment.

(a) *Financial Structure.*   When the corporate income tax in the United States reached 52 per cent in the years following World War II, and many states imposed their own taxes on corporate profits, there was a good deal of inconclusive discussion among tax economists, in and out of the Treasury, about the possible consequences for the pattern of corporate financing. Since interest paid was deductible, and dividends paid were not, corporations were afforded a golden opportunity to enhance per share earnings by issuing long-term debt, at interest rates that were still not high historically, and with the proceeds buying up their own shares on the market, or through tender offers, until the price of the shares rose to a point where no further increment in per share earnings could be obtained. This limit could not, of course, be expected to be approached closely, in view of the many nontax considerations affecting the decision with respect to the debt/equity ratio. Still, it was somewhat surprising that not a single large corporation embarked on a plan of this kind [if I recall correctly].[109]

Many years passed before a speculative boom stimulated outsiders to seize the opportunity, in connection with the conglomerate craze of the late 1960's. By issuing debt in large amounts, the new corporation—

[108] *Ibid.,* pp. 268–69.

[109] Behavior of the large corporations is what counts, in terms of aggregate effect on the economy. *Statistics of Income* for 1966, Corporation Income Tax Returns (page 63), shows that of the $77.1 billion corporate net income subject to tax, 91 corporations accounted for 29 per cent. Slightly less than half of the corporate net-income subject to tax was accounted for by the 480 largest corporations (business receipts $250,000,000 or more).

or the acquiring corporation—was able to realize so much in savings on the corporation income tax that it could offer what then appeared to be very attractive terms of exchange. Action provoked reaction, and the tax law was amended to limit, to some degree, this kind of debt issue, but there still remains an opportunity for tax saving on the part of many large corporations not involved in the conglomerate deals. I believe that this remark remains valid, even in face of the liquidity squeeze of 1970.

To be sure, the volume of corporate borrowing, relative to equity financing, did rise enough over the past two decades (excluding the conglomerates) to suggest that the tax factor was at work, especially if one accepts, even if only in part, the Modigliani-Miller thesis that in the absence of the tax, or other similar disturbing factor, investors' own portfolio adjustments should—in principle—so take account of any change in the corporations' financial structures as to leave unchanged the net worth of the firm. Yet the response of many large United States corporations to this tax differential between debt and equity financing was sluggish enough to indicate great relative importance for nontax factors.

One of these nontax factors is, of course, risk. A recent study by Luigi Tambini [110] takes into account estimated changes in riskiness of debt (lender's risk) and riskiness of equity (borrower's risk) and ex-plains away, for certain years, much of the apparent puzzle that arises when average costs of equity-financing or of debt-financing, rather than marginal costs, are considered. The "change in lender's and borrower's risk will be estimated and then added to average costs to give estimates of the corresponding marginal costs for seven bench-mark years." [111] Tambini concludes that in five of these years (1927, 1932, 1937, 1960, and 1965), manfacturing corporations "were close or very close to financial equilibrium," so that only in the other two years (1949 and 1953) does some of the puzzle remain for this group of corporations; in these two years, "the marginal cost of equity financing substantially exceeded the marginal cost of debt financing." [112]

[110] "Financial Policy and the Corporate Income Tax," in Arnold C. Harberger and Martin J. Bailey, eds., *The Taxation of Income from Capital*. Washington, D.C., The Brookings Institution, 1969, pp. 185–222. See Franco Modigliani and Merton H. Miller, "The Cost of Capital, Corporation Finance and the Theory of Investment," *American Economic Review,* Vol. 48 (June, 1958), pp. 261–97.

[111] Harberger and Bailey, *op. cit.,* p. 194. Tambini used the regression results obtained by Lawrence Fisher (debt) and Marshall Kolin (equity) as to changes in risk. State corporation income taxes are apparently not taken into account.

[112] *Ibid.,* p. 215.

In Tambini's analysis, "The basic point is that a change in financial structure affects the riskiness of corporate capital, that is, of debt and equity . . . an increase in debt financing, or leverage, increases the riskiness of the firm . . . , and therefore the risk for debt-holders (lender's risk) and the risk for stockholders (borrower's risk)." [113] Clearly, Tambini's analysis can, as he points out, be accepted only by those who are willing to follow him in differing fundamentally with Modigliani and Miller. They "postulate a net separation between variability and uncertainty of earnings," the latter referring to nonfinancial or business risk, and then consider that " 'variability over time of the successive elements of the stream [of earnings] . . . can be safely neglected. . . .' " [114] As Tambini notes, "If earnings variability can be neglected, so can 'financial risk' and therefore financial structure." [115] But in Tambini's view, "Variability of earnings would be perfectly irrelevant only if the time distribution of earnings were known with certainty." [116]

Once again the public-finance economist is forced to suspend judgment unless he is fairly sure which of the underlying, and still contested, theoretical structures he will accept (if indeed either).

There remains, of course, the largely unexplored area of the financial structure of unincorporated concerns. Here, the traditional reliance on debt-financing in some subareas, notably the housing market, might be expected to mask the effects, if any, of the tax differential in a manner just the opposite of what occurs in the corporate field. If the tax law had exempted earnings of unincorporated concerns as long as they were retained in the business, would the pattern of financing in the noncorporate sector have been appreciably different? [117]

The other major taxes in the United States seem not, by a priori reasoning, to affect appreciably the capital structure of business firms. Exceptions may be the taxes that are not linked directly with cash flows —notably the real estate tax imposed on capital value; these taxes must induce some caution in assuming still further fixed cash-outlay commitments. Do business firms with a slow rate of capital turnover—thus, by

---

[113] *Ibid.,* p. 196.
[114] *Ibid.,* p. 196, note 17.
[115] *Idem.*
[116] *Ibid.,* p. 197.
[117] Some of the findings of Seltzer are relevant to this issue; see his *Interest As a Source of Personal Income and Tax Revenue.* Occasional Paper No. 51. New York, National Bureau of Economic Research, 1955.

implication, depending more on assets of a kind subject to the real estate tax—finance themselves less with debt than do those with a rapid rate of capital turnover? In practice, it seems to be the other way around, since the very assets that attract real estate tax also serve nicely as collateral for bonds. But this statement leaves the basic question still open: How would the financing pattern change if the real estate tax were levied as a percentage of rent actually received? So far as I am aware, no quantitative studies have been made of the effect of the real estate tax (capital-value type) on business financial structure.

(b) *Methods of Wage or Salary Payment.*   Common observation suggests that in the United States the payment of wages and salaries in the form of cash has been reduced appreciably by the tax-exempt or tax-deferred status of offset income; that is, income that takes the form of a claim that a taxpayer obtains from a market transaction but which is offset, in whole or in large part, by a simultaneous obligation he incurs, or free service that he is given. (The taxpayer is operating on both sides of the market at once.) An example is supplied by good working conditions. No doubt cash wages and salaries have also been increased by the existence of poor working conditions. But the net result of the income tax itself is to put pressure on firms to improve working conditions, rather than to give an increase in cash wages or salary that would be equally satisfactory to the employee, after allowing for the tax he has to pay on it. Some evidence is at hand on the extent to which substitutes for direct cash payment have been employed, with particular reference to the income tax.[118]

Allied to payment in offset income is payment in deferred income, or in potentially tax-favored income, as through stock options.[119]

The 1969 Tax Reform Act, by setting a bracket-rate ceiling of 50 per cent on earned income, may provide occasion for a study of the effect of such tax-rate reduction on the amount of salaries and wages paid in offset income.

[118] C. Harry Kahn, *Employee Compensation Under the Income Tax.* National Bureau of Economic Research. New York, Columbia University Press, 1968, and Wilbur G. Lewellen, *Executive Compensation in Large Industrial Corporations.* National Bureau of Economic Research. New York, Columbia University Press, 1968; Hugh Holleman Macaulay, Jr., *Fringe Benefits and Their Federal Tax Treatment.* New York, Columbia University Press, 1959. See also Robert G. Rice, "An Analysis of Wage Supplements," Columbia Doctoral Dissertation, 1965.

[119] See, e.g., George E. Lent and John A. Menge, "The Importance of Restricted Stock Options in Executive Compensation," *Management Record,* Vol. 24, No. 6 (June, 1962), pp. 6–13.

D. Effects of Taxes on Supply of Labor

The effect on supply of labor that is exerted by one or another tax has usually been taken as a problem in microanalysis. The wage, or salary, rate before subtraction of tax has been assumed, or implied, to be the same as it would have been if the tax had not been in existence. The analysis then seeks to determine the worker's, or executive's, or professional's reaction to the reduction in disposable income presumably represented by the tax.

If the sector of the labor market that is being studied is small enough, this assumption, or implication, may be useful for that small sector; but to generalize from it does not seem legitimate. If the response to the question is generally that everyone would work harder in the absence of the tax, this increase in the amount of labor offered on the market might be expected to reduce the marginal productivity of labor and, hence, the real wage rate; and vice versa, of course, if the responses were the opposite. More generally, a tax on labor is to be analyzed in a nonclosed model (i.e., no specification is made of the use of the tax revenue) as is an excise tax, with effects on the amount of labor, the wage paid gross of tax, and the wage received net of tax. Friction aside, it would make no difference whether the tax were levied on the purchaser or the supplier of labor.

Moreover, if the sector being studied is indeed small and specialized, so that the individuals are analogous to oligopolist firms, an increase in a personal income tax may induce the taxpayers to react almost as a group in exploiting a hitherto unused portion of their oligopoly power.

A few examples of recent studies of the effect of taxation on effort will illustrate these points. George Break's personal interviews with 306 solicitors and accountants in England were evidently carried on under an assumption that if the income tax were removed, or lowered, their fees would not be lowered by the increased amount of that kind of labor that would be put on the market (or would not be raised, if the effect were the opposite).[120] The same is true of Davidson's conclusions from interviews with a few high-earning surgeons,[121] and also of the sample

[120] G. F. Break, "Income Taxes and Incentives to Work: an Empirical Study," *American Economic Review* (Sept., 1957), pp. 529–49. Break found that there was no rise in the incidence of tax disincentives in this presumably tax-sensitive group, from that found in the study of workers (see second note below). *Loc. cit.*, p. 548.

[121] Robert Davidson, "Income Taxes and Incentive: the Doctor's Viewpoint," *National Tax Journal* (Sept., 1953), pp. 293–97.

survey carried out in the early 1950's on behalf of the Royal Commission on the Taxation of Profits and Income, in which a large majority of the 1,429 workers interviewed said they thought the income tax's disincentive influence tended to reduce output.[122]

The questions asked recently of the United States business executives encounter the same problem. If, for example, executives assure us that under lower taxes they would work more, which presumably implies more striving in the younger years and less premature retirement, they are saying that the substitution effect of the tax outweighs the income effect. If we were then to point out that their lifetime pay ex tax would fall as more of their labor was put on the market, they would, in principle, have to compare a new set of income and substitution effects, each of them now stronger than before this macro element was taken into account. Even then, as noted above, the question will not have been put in general-equilibrium terms—or rather, in terms of a closed model —since it will not have been specified how the government would make good the loss of revenue.

These cautionary remarks do not imply that such micro-based studies are valueless, quite the contrary. They are the necessary, and often laborious and difficult, first steps in attacking the problem of the effect of taxation on labor effort. The many insights that are gathered with respect to the individual's reaction to taxation are exemplified in the recent research project carried on by Daniel M. Holland,[123] through his one- to two-hour interviews with 122 top business executives [124] in the United States (together with some less formal individual and group discussions). Holland emphasized the income effects of the income tax by asking his interviewees to consider how differently they would have acted under a tax with the same income effect but without any substitution

[122] *Second Report*. London, HMSO, 1954, p. 108; noted by Break, *op. cit.,* p. 529.

[123] Daniel M. Holland, "The Effect of Taxation on Effort: Some Results for Business Executives." Preliminary draft of a paper presented at the National Tax Conference of 1969, to be published in that conference's Proceedings. (Page references are to the mimeographed document.) Effort spent on investment decisions and the effects of death-gift taxes were included in some of the discussions. *Ibid.,* pp. 15–17. This project was supported by the National Bureau of Economic Research.

[124] Thirty-three of them were chief executives of large companies, 21 were chief executives of smaller companies, 46 were middle managers, 17 represented a cross-section of businessmen in two rapidly growing cities, and 5 were men of technical or scientific background with academic interests. *Ibid.,* pp. 3–5.

effect (a tax on potential income, not an ordinary poll tax).[125] But, as had the others in preceding studies, he abstracted from any effect on pre-tax salary that might be exerted from a change in the supply of effort, either through macroeffects on the labor market, or through exploitation of unused oligopoly power.

Holland's study cannot be adequately summarized here; but the chief finding, from the viewpoint of the present section, was that "the weight of the evidence is consistent with the conclusions based on other evidence from my own interviews and from earlier studies—most executives, indeed by far the largest proportion, are working about as hard as they can despite prevailing levels of income taxation [compared with what would happen under a tax on potential income]." [126] And "not one of the 18 top executives in very large companies felt that he would be induced to work any harder at his job by so basic a change in the tax law [i.e., to a tax on potential income]." [127] But some exceptions were found among chief executives of smaller companies, and among managers.

W. B. Reddaway's recently issued Volume One of his study of the effects of the British Selective Employment Tax (SET) [128] explicitly recognizes the need to specify what else would have happened had the tax not been introduced. He will specify an alternative tax,[129] but in this initial report he defers consideration of that aspect.

Marvin Kosters [130] has extended the macro approach (i.e., specifying the use made of the revenue), but remains on the intermediate level

[125] *Ibid.*, pp. 12, 18–20.

[126] *Ibid.*, p. 22.

[127] *Ibid.*, pp. 23–24.

[128] W. B. Reddaway, *Effects of the Selective Employment Tax, First Report: The Distribution Trades.* London, HMSO, 1970.

[129] "In 1966, SET was introduced as a net addition to taxation rather than in replacement of some other form of tax. Nevertheless, we conceive our task as being to assess what the effects of SET are, *as against having some alternative tax in its place,* or an increase in the level of some other tax. The nature and size of this alternative taxation needs very careful exposition, which will not be attempted until we produce our Final Report covering the whole research." This alternative tax would be presumed to have the same "consequences for the over-all balance of demand and potential supply for goods and services taken as a whole . . . [but] no *special* effect on the trades which are unable to recover SET, or on the consumers of their products. . . ." A general tax on value-added is mentioned as a possible alternative. *Ibid.*, p. 3.

[130] "Effects of an Income Tax on Labor Supply," in Harberger and Bailey, eds., *op. cit.,* pp. 301–324.

(i.e., assuming no change in the pretax wage rate), by stipulating, in one part of his study, that an increase in income tax is used to supply the workers with free government services of equal value. From empirical evidence on wage-rate effects, he concludes that the resulting "change in labor supply . . . induced by the [income-] compensated wage rate effect" is "likely to be very small" for male primary workers, while for married women "an increase in the tax rate which results in a given percentage decrease in the net wage rate might be accompanied by as much as an equal percentage decline in the labor force participation rate." Kosters also notes that "a change in the income tax rate is likely to have a smaller effect on labor supplied by a family than is suggested by estimates derived from wage rate changes," since "a single tax rate applied to a family when a joint return is filed . . . provides no incentive for substitution between family members. . . ." [131]

E. Excess Burden from Taxation

Although the literature on excess burden in public finance is vast, quantitative estimates seem not to have been attempted before Arnold C. Harberger's 1955 contribution on the welfare loss caused by excessive depletion and similar allowances.[132] His subsequent contributions, to be noted below, appear to have been the only ones of their kind published until the 1969 volume of which he was coeditor.[133] This lack of participation by the profession is difficult to account for, except that worry over the quantitative aspects of excess burden is difficult to arouse among lawmakers, or, for that matter, anyone but economists.

Excess burden, as that term is used here, refers to the reduction in welfare that occurs under the pressure exerted on individuals and business firms by a tax, a subsidy, or a free government service: the pressure being to substitute one pattern of action for another, otherwise more

[131] *Ibid.*, p. 323. As an alternative to the government services, Kosters, of course, offers an equal-yield tax which has no effect on the labor supply.

[132] "The Taxation of Mineral Industries in the United States," in U.S. Congress, Joint Committee on the Economic Report, *Federal Tax Policy for Economic Growth*. Washington, D.C., Superintendent of Documents, 1955, pp. 439–49. See also Susan R. Agria, "Special Tax Treatment of Mineral Industries," in Harberger and Bailey, eds., *op. cit.*, pp. 77–122, where it is estimated that "there is an incentive to invest about 1.5 times as much capital to produce a given income stream in oil exploration and development as in another industry not accorded the depletion and expensing privileges . . ." (p. 96). "For coal, there is incentive to invest around 1.8 times as much capital as in a normal industry" (p. 98).

[133] See note 110 above.

acceptable to the actor, simply to change thereby the amount of tax; and so on. (In the end, the actor—or, at least, the actors in the aggregate —do not gain even that satisfaction, since the tax rates, for example, are raised to obviate the loss in revenue.) The action affected may be the choice of a pattern of consumption (including leisure as an element in consumption), or the choice of a technique of production. The results of acting in such fashion are compared with the hypothetical results under some neutral tax of equivalent revenue. Here, *neutral* means that the amount of the neutral tax due does not change if the taxpayer alters his choice among the patterns of consumption or production. This is true, for example, of a head tax, which is indeed neutral with respect to all types of action, save emigration or suicide. A uniform-rate tax on the return from all capital *is,* while a corporation income tax *is not,* neutral with respect to (*a*) the pattern in which total production is carried on as between the corporate and noncorporate sectors, and (*b*) methods of finance.

Harberger's estimates [134] obviously had to employ assumptions about elasticities of demand and substitutability in production, but the ones he selected seem plausible enough to make the estimates worth taking seriously (unit elasticities of demand, Cobb-Douglas production functions). The amounts of excess burden involved, though perhaps not large enough to weigh heavily with unconcerned policy-makers, certainly deserve attention. For the corporate income tax, Harberger estimated an excess burden of about $1.5 billion a year as of 1953–55; this figure would presumably be much larger as of 1970.[135] For the individual income tax, he estimated some $1 billion a year of excess burden

[134] "The Corporation Income Tax: An Empirical Appraisal," in U.S. Congress, Committee on Ways and Means, *Tax Revision Compendium.* Washington, D.C., Superintendent of Documents, 1959, Vol. 1, pp. 231–50; and "Taxation, Resource Allocation, and Welfare," in National Bureau of Economic Research and Brookings Institution Conference Report, *The Role of Direct and Indirect Taxation in the Federal Revenue System.* Princeton University Press, 1964, pp. 25–70, and Comment by E. Cary Brown and William Fellner.

[135] *Op. cit.,* 1959, p. 235. Leonard Gerson Rosenberg, "Taxation of Income from Capital, by Industry Group," in Harberger and Bailey, eds., *op. cit.,* estimates the net cost of distortion from the corporation income tax and the property tax, 1959 ($20 billion corporate profits tax, $14 billion property taxes), at some $600 million. Rosenberg notes that "it is plausible to assume that the property tax does tend to offset the distorting effect of the corporate profits tax on the corporate sector." *Ibid.,* p. 179. He does not compute the distortion cost for the corporate profits tax separately, but does distribute the distortion cost of both taxes together, industry by industry.

from the inducement to work less, than under an equal-yield tax that did not lower the cost of leisure.[136] To this, he added another $1 billion to account for the pressure exerted by the income tax toward present consumption at the cost of larger future consumption, compared with a tax that did not thus change the terms of trade between present and future.[137] Finally, we must add the estimates for excess burden created by tax preferences for one or another industry. Harberger estimated that percentage depletion and its related provisions cost between $0.5 and $1.0 billion a year in welfare,[138] and cited a study by Laidler giving about the same range of welfare loss from the income tax exemption of net imputed rent on owner-occupied housing.[139]

Taking all of these estimates together, and intuitively updating them to 1970, suggests that the excess burden of the federal revenue system (to say nothing of the state and local tax systems) might well be of the order of some $10 billion a year. Two obvious next steps in quantitative work are: (1) to extend the estimates to state and local taxes; and (2) to ascertain how much of this total welfare loss could be recouped by altering the United States tax system in a manner not obviously unacceptable for other reasons.

A third step, although equally obvious, poses more formidable problems of computation. It arises from the need to take account of the theory of second-best. From James Meade, we learn that in a world where the excess burden in question is not the only instance of divergence between marginal values and true costs, "the reduction of one of these divergences—the others remaining unchanged—will not necessarily lead to an increase in economic welfare, but may very well reduce it." Paraphrasing one of Meade's illustrations, we may postulate that if, for example, in two industries turning out highly substitutable products (say, rail transport service and highway transport service) such divergences exist—owing to special taxes on each of the two industries (the proceeds not being devoted to supply infrastructure for them)—the divergence being considerably higher in the one (say, rail transport)

[136] Op. cit., 1964, p. 51.

[137] Op. cit., 1964, p. 61.

[138] Op. cit., 1955, pp. 439–49.

[139] This study was published, in 1969, in Harberger and Bailey, eds., op. cit., David Laidler, "Income Tax Incentives for Owner-Occupied Housing," pp. 50–76. Laidler's minimum estimate of the welfare cost "of the failure to levy the income tax on the service accruing to owner-occupiers" is somewhat more than $500 million a year. Ibid., p. 63.

than in the other, a reduction of the divergence in the latter (highway transport) by a reduction in the special tax on such transport might decrease total welfare.[140]

A more general statement of the theory of second-best was later developed by R. G. Lipsey and Kelvin Lancaster: ". . . given that one of the Paretian optimum conditions cannot be fulfilled, then an optimum situation can be achieved only by departing from all the other Paretian conditions." [141] Lipsey and Lancaster concede that Meade's approach, which "deals with a system containing many constraints and investigates the optimum (second-best) level for one of them, assuming the invariability of all the others," is "probably the appropriate one when considering problems of actual policy in a world where many imperfections exist and only a few can be removed at any one time," in contrast to their approach, which is to "assume the existence of [only] one [such] constraint . . . and then to investigate the nature of the conditions that must be satisfied in order to achieve a second-best optimum. . . ." [142]

The problem thus appears to be whether a particular quantitative estimate of the amount to be gained in welfare by eliminating one specific divergence is seriously, or only negligibly, affected by the existence of the large number of other important divergences in the economic system. Harberger, while calling attention to the problem of second-best, has not attempted to allow for it in the quantitative estimates noted above.[143]

F. Time Series and Cross-Section Studies of Tax System Characteristics

Since the development of a tax system over time in any one country has commonly been studied to help answer one or more of the questions presented here under other headings, and since the same may be said of comparative studies across countries, there is only a limited value in the

[140] J. E. Meade, *Trade and Welfare.* London, Oxford University Press, 1955, p. 102.

[141] "The General Theory of Second-Best," *Review of Economic Studies,* Vol. XXIV(1), No. 63 (1956–57), p. 11.

[142] *Ibid.,* p. 13.

[143] "The Measurement of Waste," *American Economic Review,* Vol. LIV, No. 3 (May, 1964), p. 59. See, in this connection, the remarks by Dale E. Jorgenson, Tjalling C. Koopmans, and Paul A. Samuelson, in "Discussion," *ibid.,* pp. 87–88, p. 93, and pp. 93–95, respectively; and Karl Roskamp's review of Harberger and Bailey, *op. cit., Journal of Finance* (June, 1970), pp. 737–38.

present section as a separate unit of discussion. This is particularly so if, as I have done, the much-debated issue of a possible maximum ratio of taxation to national income, or *GNP,* is postponed to the section dealing directly with the search for "laws" of government expenditure (III-G below).

There remain, chiefly, the studies of differences in structures of tax systems, either in one country over time, or among countries. For example, how do the tax systems—each system taken as a whole—compare over time, or among countries, with respect to the proportion taken in indirect taxes (I should prefer the term *impersonal taxes,* i.e., taxes the rates of which depend little, if at all, on the personal attributes of anyone)? Or how do they differ with respect to the distribution of taxing power among levels of government; with respect to the treatment of the poor, the elderly, the large family, the farmer; or with respect to domestic capital abroad, and foreign capital at home? [144]

Furthermore, even when such questions have been answered, what do they tell us? Too often the information is hardly more useful, directly, than data on the proportion of taxation imposed on inhabitants over six feet in height. Frequently, the reader seems to be expected to supply his own reasons for wanting to know what proportion of the tax revenue arises from "indirect" taxes, or for wanting to know whether this proportion varies, for example, with income per capita.

The most important exceptions to the foregoing charge are the recent works by Musgrave [145] and by Pryor,[146] and the Proceedings of

---

[144] A comparison of progressivity of an entire tax system of one country with that of another country is useful in the differential sense described in Section II-A above, but only if the differences are gross enough to suggest that a transfer of the tax system of Country A to Country B would yield results in Country B, relative to those observed under B's existing system, much the same as it does yield in Country A. If, for example, the price elasticity of supply of highly paid executives is much greater in A than in B (perhaps because in A such persons can more easily migrate to similar jobs in other countries), and if A's existing tax system is, according to its rate schedule, much more progressive at the salary levels of these executives than is that of B, it would be a mistake to think of A's system as being really much more progressive than B's. A's executives, those that remain in Country A, will have recouped part, or all, of the higher progressivity through tax-induced higher salaries.

[145] Richard A. Musgrave, *Fiscal Systems.* New Haven, Yale University Press, 1969, Chapters 5–7.

[146] Frederic L. Pryor, *Public Expenditures in Communist and Capitalist Nations.* Homewood, Ill., Irwin, 1968.

the conference held by The Brookings Institution and the National Bureau: "Foreign Tax Policies and Economic Growth." [147]

Musgrave poses a theory of the circumstances governing the ratio of direct to indirect taxes. He then concludes that the empirical evidence is "well in line with expectations." [148] The evidence consists, first, of a historical study of the development of the tax structures in selected countries (United Kingdom, United States, and Germany); and second, a cross-sectional study of thirty to forty countries. The expectations fulfilled are, however, only those that are expressed in terms both so general and so obvious that if the evidence had contradicted the expectations, one would have been tempted to suspect the evidence, not the expectations. Some of the more detailed parts of the expectational section are not covered by the data and—if they had been—would, I think, have been contradicted here and there in a manner that would open all kinds of interesting inquiries: for example, the proportion of tax revenue raised by taxes on land in the less developed countries. The cross-sectional data are broken down only into indirect taxes (including customs duties), customs duties listed separately, corporation income tax, personal income tax, and social security taxes.

Pryor, in his monumental cross-sectional study of government expenditures, tests, by regressions, for effect of tax structure on expenditures, but finds no statistically significant relationships, except that between total direct personal taxes and expenditures, which he concludes "seems to reflect the discovery of Aaron . . . that social insurance expenditures are related to tied taxes." [149]

The Brookings-Bureau study on tax structures and economic growth illustrates another difficulty in drawing boundaries that will include only quantitative studies. Although these conference papers are essentially descriptions of tax structures, with emphasis on tax measures taken with the aim of promoting economic growth, and although they, therefore, contain neither a priori models nor data for testing such models, they are helpful to the public-finance scholar in ways additional to those supplied by Musgrave's regressions. They suggest new quantitative insights, open new avenues to explore, and stimulate that untidy mixture of introspection, general observation, and intuition on which most of us probably still rely, in the main.

[147] See note 86 above.
[148] Musgrave, *op. cit.*, pp. 155–56.
[149] *Op. cit.*, p. 440.

III. GOVERNMENT EXPENDITURES

G. The Search for "Laws" of Government Expenditures

Quantitative studies of government expenditures fall chiefly into two groups. In one, the studies have sought to ascertain whether there is a tendency in the private-enterprise economies, as distinguished from the socialist economies, for per capita government-expenditures to rise over time faster than per capita national income or per capita *GNP*. The second group of studies has attempted to isolate the influence of each of many variables in addition to per capita income: degree of urbanization, amount of aid received from higher-level governments, and the like. They have been concerned usually with states and local units, particularly cities, rather than with country-to-country comparisons.

(1) **Variation of Government Expenditures with Per Capita Income.** The first group of studies take off from Wagner's somewhat ambiguous assertion, which has become known as the law of increasing government expenditures. Wagner's data, on the whole, may not have indicated much more than the likelihood that, as per capita income rises, government expenditure per capita rises at least as rapidly.[150] In recent years, cross-section studies comparing countries with differing per capita incomes at a given time have been attempted, in order to answer indirectly the question of variation over time; though it is recognized that today countries are subject to worldwide cultural, and other influences, which make cross-section conclusions not particularly comparable with those drawn from a time series for one country.

Recently, however, the field of inquiry has been remarkably widened by Pryor's cross-section study, which compares private-enterprise economies with socialist economies, and compares the structure of services rendered by government in the various countries. (See paragraph below.)

Of the time-series studies, the most provocative and potentially important is the Peacock-Wiseman analysis of United Kingdom government expenditures from 1890 to the post-World War II period.[151] Their conclusion that crisis periods, notably war, condition taxpayers to a

---

[150] For a detailed critique of Wagner's "law" see Herbert Timm, "Das Gesetz der wachsenden Staatsausgaben," *Finanzarchiv*, Vol. 21, No. 2 (Sept., 1961), pp. 201–47.

[151] A. T. Peacock and J. Wiseman, *The Growth of Public Expenditures in the United Kingdom.* National Bureau of Economic Research. Princeton University Press, 1961.

level of taxes that continues to be acceptable—particularly if per capita incomes are rising, and if social consciences have been stirred by war's hardships—in a postwar period for additions to peaceful types of government expenditures is indeed plausible; although I have argued elsewhere [152] that "at some points the displacement effect seems to be defined implicitly in terms, not of share of government expediture in *GNP,* but of government expenditure per head (after deflating for price changes)." [153] In any case, in projecting U.K. government expenditures, Peacock and Wiseman sensibly make no use of the displacement hypothesis, on the implicit assumption that there will not again be a war like World War II. The assumptions they do use in their projections give a result that implies that the U.K. will devote a strikingly large proportion of incremental *GNP* to private uses.[154] Further work now in process in this field may clarify some of these issues.[155]

Cross-section studies (Pryor aside) [see paragraph below] have become successively more discouraging in their search for some relationship between the government's share in the national income and the country's per capita income. Musgrave's cross-section analysis [156] led him to conclude that, that share—at least, for current expenditures as distinct from capital expenditures—rises with per capita *GNP* for his sample as a whole; but that the relation breaks down for the subsample of countries with per capita incomes below $300, and for those with per capita incomes of above $600 (where it even becomes negative). Finally, the most recent and extensive study for developing countries, covering forty-six countries with per capita *GNP* ranging from $38 (Malawi) to $661 (Japan), has given disappointing results. Out of the 222 correla-

[152] In a review of the Peacock-Wiseman book appearing in *The British Tax Review* (March-April, 1962), pp. 126–27. See Pryor's test of the displacement effect, and his critique, which focuses on government expenditure per capita, *op. cit.,* pp. 443–46.

[153] Shoup, *loc. cit.,* p. 126.

[154] *Ibid.,* p. 127.

[155] See J. Veverka, "The Growth of Government Expenditure in the United Kingdom since 1790," in Alan T. Peacock and D. J. Robertson, eds., *Public Expenditure: Appraisal and Control.* London, Oliver & Boyd, 1963; and by the same author, "The Growth of Government Expenditure in the United Kingdom in the 19th Century," *Scottish Journal of Political Economy,* Vol. X, No. 1, 1963 (reprinted for private circulation by the London School of Economics and Political Science, the University of London, and the Department of Economics, University of York), pp. 111–127.

[156] *Fiscal Systems,* pp. 110–24. See also the other works in this field cited by Musgrave, p. 110, note 11.

tions tried, only 13 were found significant at the 10 per cent level in relating per capita *GNP* to government expenditures or subdivisions thereof—expressed as a percentage of *GNP;* or, for particular services, as a percentage of total government expenditure.[157]

These inconclusive results may prove quite useful in forcing us to inquire more carefully into cultural factors and economic patterns that are not well reflected in simple figures of per capita income, but which doubtless affect the share of government in the economy.

The Colin Clark 25 per cent limit on the over-all tax rate,[158] derived by him from somewhat scanty data a good many years ago, is closely allied to the issue of the government's share in total output. His hypothesis that, once past the 25 per cent limit, the society opts for inflationary financing rather than more taxes, suggests that there is a similar limit of about the same size on the government's share, however financed. But the persistence of inflationary financing in many countries in peacetime shows that the concept of a tax-limit ratio is not necessarily the same, in its practical consequences, as the concept of a limit to the government's share in total output. If there is such a share-limit, it is, I think, more likely to be determined by whether the government supplies, chiefly, services to business firms or, mainly, services directly to consumers. The limit may, in principle, be very high indeed in the former case.[159]

Pryor's book is in a class by itself in the field now under discussion. An accurate appraisal of his findings will take some time, so ambitious and extensive is his coverage. The basic question is, therefore, the degree to which the limitations of the data available to him render the regression findings overly subject to qualification. But even if that were to turn out to be so, the book would still be important, owing to the manner in which Pryor has spelled out the problems of interpreting the data, has discussed the various types of government services, and has offered other qualitative analyses of his quantitative project.

Taking public consumption expenditures (which excludes public investment expenditures, government subsidies, and sales by government organs to the population), Pryor compares seven "market" economies

[157] S. Lall, "A Note on Government Expenditures in Developing Countries," *Economic Journal* (June, 1969), pp. 413–17.

[158] "Public Finance and the Value of Money," *Economic Journal* (Dec., 1945), pp. 371–89. For a critique of Clark's theory, see Joseph A. Pechman and Thomas Mayer, "Mr. Colin Clark on the Limits of Taxation," *Review of Economics and Statistics* (Aug., 1952), pp. 232–42.

[159] Carl S. Shoup, *Public Finance,* pp. 497–98.

and seven "centrally planned" economies with respect to the share of *GNP* taken in these expenditures; and in certain types of these expenditures—notably expenditures for defense, for welfare and health, and for education. The differences between the private-enterprise economies and (in my terminology) the socialist economies are not great: probably much smaller than most people, perhaps most economists, would have thought.[160]

(2) Variation of Government Expenditures with Variables Other than Per Capita Income.   Since per capita income seems, at best, to have a very limited explanatory power for differences in government spending as a share in total spending, it is encouraging to see that the initial attempts to add other explanatory variables—by Fabricant in 1952,[161] for interstate differences in the United States; and the similarly pioneering study by Brazer in 1959,[162] for intercity differences—have been followed by a considerable number of regression studies in the 1960's, which search for further associative or causal factors. But most of these studies do not pose directly the question of the government's share in total output; they ask, rather, how may a dollar increase in per capita government-expenditure be explained? It might be "completely explained" by variation in per capita income, yet the share of government in the total output might be rising, falling, or remaining constant. Fabricant employed per capita income, urbanization (percentage of population in communities of over 2,500) and density of population, and found that they accounted for a little over 70 per cent of the variance among states in per capita total expenditures,[163] income being overwhelmingly the most important factor. What made Fabricant's study of special interest was his breakdown by major types of government service, where substantial explanatory differences were found. Thus, expenditures per capita on fire protection, sanitation, and welfare were influenced chiefly by urbanization, not by income, or by density, which never ranked higher than second, and then only for schools and health and hospitals.[164]

[160] For a summary of Pryor's findings, and a critique, see the review of his book by Ronald B. Gold, *The Journal of Finance* (Dec., 1969), pp. 1032–34.

[161] Solomon Fabricant, assisted by Robert E. Lipsey, *The Trend of Government Activity in the United States since 1900*. New York, National Bureau of Economic Research, 1952, pp. 122–29.

[162] Harvey E. Brazer, *City Expenditures in the United States*. Occasional Paper 66. New York, National Bureau of Economic Research, 1959.

[163] *Op. cit.,* p. 123.

[164] *Ibid.,* p. 130.

What Fabricant had done for interstate differences, Brazer did for intercity differences, in somewhat more detail. First, he took account of a number of social and economic forces, without attempting to attach precise explanatory power to each of these, by dividing his 462 cities (all but 19 of the total in 1951 with populations over 25,000) into seven groups, defined by the characteristics of core-city, large and small metropolitan area, high and low income residential suburb, industrial suburb, city outside a metropolitan area, and resort city. Variance analysis indicated a systematic association between per capita expenditures and the "nature, or type classification, of the city." [165]

Second, Brazer applied multiple regression analysis to the 462 cities, to those of the group in each of three states (California, Massachusetts, and Ohio), and to 40 cities of over 250,000 population, with their overlapping local governments. The explanatory variables included two employed by Fabricant (density of population, and income—but median family income, rather than per capita income) and four others: population size; rate of population growth; ratio of employment in manufacturing, trade, and service to population; and intergovernmental revenue per capita. The variables to be explained were: 1951 per capita total general operating expenditures; and operating expenditures per capita for police and fire protection, streets and highways, recreation, general control, sanitation, and the combined common functions. Obviously, we are here far advanced in degree of detail from the studies noted above that compare countries, but we are still not dealing directly with variations in the share of the community's total output taken by government.

The chief explanatory variables turned out to be density, median family income, and intergovernmental revenue per capita. (This summary, of necessity, omits many important details discovered by Brazer.) In the 40-city study, where three additional explanatory variables were used, Brazer found that "the smaller the proportion of the metropolitan area's population that lives in the central city, the higher its per capita expenditures tend to be." [166]

The field opened up by Fabricant and Brazer was rapidly exploited in the 1960's, as computers became more available, and as state-local fiscal difficulties increased, especially at the urban level. More than any

[165] Harvey B. Brazer, "Factors Affecting City Expenditures," *Proceedings, Fiftieth Annual Conference on Taxation,* National Tax Association, 1957, p. 440. For citation of the complete study, see footnote 162 above.
[166] *Ibid.,* p. 443.

other area of public finance, this field is now in what might be called a theoretic quantitative flux. Monographs and articles have followed hard on one another, each challenging the findings of its predecessor(s), especially with respect to the response of state and local governments to grants from a higher-level government. It is not possible to summarize here the intricate developments in the literature contributed by Barlow, Bolton, Gramlich, Harris, Oates, Osman, Sacks, Thurow, and others, but two aspects recently emphasized may be singled out as being important technically.[167]

First, the conclusion reached in some of the studies, that considerable influence on government spending can be attributed to receipt of grants in aid, may have to be reconsidered in those cases where this explanatory variable is expressed in absolute terms (either as total amount, or total per capita), instead of as a proportion of total local expenditure. For example, even in the absence of any causal effect running from aid to local spending, one would expect a richer state to exhibit both a larger local expenditure per capita, and a larger amount of state aid to local units per capita.

Second, as the search for explanatory variables has widened, the danger arises that for any particular cross-section-analysis set of data, some set of assumed causal agents can be found that will, in toto, seem to explain the variations in local spending, but that in reality show a good deal of chance association, rather than causality. This danger arises from the fact that, until recently, these studies have lacked an a priori behavioral-definitional model to be tested. This gap is being overcome with the aid of models that set up utility functions for the governments in question, to be maximized subject to certain types of budget restraint.[168]

[167] The immediately following paragraphs are based to a considerable degree on the analysis and findings of Stephen Dresch, of the National Bureau of Economic Research. See also the forthcoming volume by Dresch and Raymond Struyk. Neither of these authors is responsible for the paraphrasing and comments in this text.

[168] See, especially, the empirical work of Edward M. Gramlich, "State and Local Governments and Their Budget Constraint," *International Economic Review*, Vol. 10, No. 2 (June, 1969), pp. 163–82; his "Alternative Federal Policies for Stimulating State and Local Expenditures: A Comparison of Their Effects," *National Tax Journal*, Vol. 21, No. 2 (June, 1968), pp. 119–29; and "A Clarification and a Correction," *National Tax Journal*, Vol. 22, No. 2 (June, 1969), pp. 286–90. On the theoretical side, see James A. Wilde, "The Expenditure Effects of Grants-in-Aid Programs," *National Tax Journal*, Vol. 21, No. 3 (Sept., 1968), pp. 340–48.

H. Trends and Time Series of Government Expenditures in Particular Countries

The studies of trends and time series of government expenditures that are the subject of this section differ from those discussed in Section G (above) in that they seek less for specific causal relationships and more for a general understanding of the changing level and structure of government expenditure, whatever the causes. It is correspondingly more difficult to summarize or appraise these studies, and the present section merely calls attention to some of the more significant of them: those by Fabricant (already noted in another context),[169] Kendrick and Wehle,[170] and Andic and Veverka [171] (without implying that those not noted here are all of less significance).[172]

These studies deal, inter alia, with trends in the number of government employees and their distribution among the several government functions,[173] recognizing, of course, that trends in government employment can be different—even opposite in sign—from total government expenditures.

I. Quantitative Aspects of Government Services as Distinguished from Government Expenditures (Output, as Distinguished from Money Input)

There are few data, and little in the way of conceptual analysis concerning government services, i.e., government output, as distinguished from government expenditures—which are simply figures on money input. Time-series and cross-section studies of amounts spent, total or per capita, on education, police, and other services, tell us, by themselves, nothing about the level of the service rendered, since the data are

[169] See footnote 161 above.

[170] M. Slade Kendrick, assisted by Mark Wehle, *A Century and a Half of Federal Expenditures*. Occasional Paper 48. National Bureau of Economic Research, 1955.

[171] Suphan Andic and Jindrich Veverka, "The Growth of Government Expenditure in Germany Since the Unification," *Finanzarchiv*, Vol. 23, No. 2 (Jan., 1964), pp. 169–278.

[172] For an extensive bibliography on recent empirical studies of public expenditures, see Pryor, *op. cit.,* pp. 446–51.

[173] For particular studies of this point, see Solomon Fabricant, *The Rising Trend of Government Employment*. Occasional Paper 29. National Bureau of Economic Research. New York, 1949; and M. Abramovitz and Vera F. Eliasberg, *Growth of Public Employment in Great Britain*. National Bureau of Economic Research. Princeton University Press, 1957.

only for inputs. We lack, on the whole, analogues to the physical units found in much of the private sector (tons of coal, numbers of trucks of a certain specification), because government output—at least, that part distributed free of charge—consists almost entirely of services, not commodities. But we lack also the dollar-sales figures of the kind available for services supplied in the private sector, which reflect consumer demand, and which, therefore, are an aid to measuring the output of an industry, say, retail trade.

This general observation is not invalidated by the wealth of cost-benefit studies that have marked the past few decades in the United States. Most of these studies have been concerned with marketable types of output, not group-consumption goods (nonexclusion goods). Also, the outputs have been definable in physical units. Value per unit has been assigned by reference to private-sector analogues, or by observing the reduction in costs they make possible in the private-sector activity that uses them, since most of these government services in cost-benefit analyses have been intermediate goods. When the same technique has been applied, sometimes under the name of PPB (program-planning-budgeting, which actually embraces much more than cost-benefit analysis), to those government departments dispensing pure public goods, e.g., the State Department, it has there proved unworkable or extremely difficult to apply, as a method of ascertaining cost per unit of output. Cost comparison of alternative methods of accomplishing a specified task is, of course, possible even in these cases, but this bypasses the problem of defining units of output.

For these reasons, most of the cost-benefit analyses have seemed to me to lie outside the discipline of public finance, at any rate as I am inclined to define it: namely, one of the economy's resource-allocating systems that makes little use of the pricing mechanism in drawing resources from the economy and reallocating them through free services and transfer payments.[174]

The same remarks are applicable to services that the government, although supplying them free of direct charge, dispenses in the marketing mode, i.e., a mode whereby the amount of the service in question can be rationed, consumer by consumer, and is in fact so rationed—though by direct rationing, rather than by the impersonal price system. Education and garbage removal are examples. Government renders these services in this mode because they produce externalities (e.g., im-

[174] See Shoup, *Public Finance*, pp. 3–5.

proved milieu) that are not marketable, and partly as a means of redistributing wealth and income. The basic services, education, garbage removal, and the like, while differing among themselves in the ease with which a unit of output can be defined, do not offer the difficulties inherent in defining a unit of output of a service rendered in the group-consumption (nonexcludability) mode, where exclusion of any particular individual is not feasible: for example, police protection, fire protection, and (now we deal with collective-consumption goods, where the addition of one more consumer to the group does not change total cost) defense, public health, and exploration of space. Accordingly, although we have some definitions of unit of output, and quantitative studies of cost per unit, for free services rendered in the marketing mode,[175] there is relatively little of either for those government services supplied in the nonmarketing mode.[176]

J. Changes in Efficiency in the Government Sector

This section is included in the present monograph more for its intrinsic interest as a quantitative problem yet to be solved than for the attempts made thus far to grapple with it. That these attempts have

[175] See, e.g., J. A. Kershaw and R. N. McKean, *Systems Analysis and Education*. Santa Monica, Calif., Rand, 1959; some of the papers in Howard G. Schaller, ed., *Public Expenditure Decisions in the Urban Community*. Baltimore, Johns Hopkins Press, 1963, especially those by Werner Z. Hirsch; and Werner Z. Hirsch, *The Economics of State and Local Government*. New York, McGraw-Hill, 1970.

[176] See, however, Burton A. Weisbrod, *Economics of Public Health*. Philadelphia, University of Pennsylvania Press, 1963; and, for concepts of output, Shoup, *Public Finance*, pp. 102–27. A promising empirical study recently completed is that by Raul Treviño-Westendarp, "On the Distribution of Free Governmental Services: Police Protection in New York City." New York, Columbia University; Doctoral Dissertation, 1970. Treviño-Westendarp deals with definition and measurement of crime, units of output, police deployment, and the degree to which the deployment in New York City, as given for a single date (no other data are publicly available) would, if continued, resemble the deployments that would occur under each of three potentially conflicting criteria for deployment: equal crime rates in all precincts, minimum crime rate for the City as a whole, and equal work-load. Owing to the unwillingness of the police department to release data on deployment, this study chiefly indicates how these quantitative aspects could be examined, rather than itself providing definitive answers with respect to the results of differing deployment patterns (deployment by area, and by time periods during the day). Similar questions are raised, and data are obtained that give partial answers, in Sam Book, "Taxation of Commuters in New York City." New York, Columbia University; Doctoral Dissertation, 1969. See Section V below.

been few and inconclusive is to be expected from what has been noted in Section I (above) about lack of data, or even concepts, on units of output. Efficiency rises when a government succeeds in increasing the number of units of output of a certain service from a given money value of input. Without a definition of a unit of output, changes in efficiency cannot be measured even conceptually.

But trends over time can perhaps be implied, as Fabricant attempted to do, by his "intuitive weighing of changes that tend to decrease productivity, e.g., decline in hours worked per week (if 'input' is measured not in man-hours but in man-weeks) and those that tend to increase productivity, e.g., apparently favorable changes in administrative methods. . . . On this basis Fabricant . . . concludes that for the period 1900–1940, 'The net result probably has been a decline in input relative to output.' " [177]

IV. NEEDS AND PROSPECTS FOR RESEARCH

The following appraisal of the needs, prospects, and outlets for quantitative research in government expenditures and taxation (based on the summaries above) is offered as a personal, subjective reaction, liable to change upon discussion. Still, in order to avoid cumbersome repetition, the propositions below will be stated almost as flatly as if they were revealed truths.

1. Each quantitative study will say whether: (1) it employs off-the-shelf data to illustrate or suggest a new, or a modified, theory of causal relationships; or (2) it obtains a set of observations in a manner designed to test a theory that has been developed without reference to these observations; or (3) it brings together data that, under correlation or regression analysis, reveal associations that may prove useful for policy guidance, even though there is no a priori model that would help reveal the particular causal relations, if any (black-box empiricism). The distinction between (2) and (3) is illustrated by the differences described in Section II-B (above) of the various studies on shifting and incidence.

The Type 3 study (no a priori model) will, no doubt, continue to be used in some fields where a priori models are very difficult to construct, notably in the study of historical and cross-sectional differences in levels and structures of public expenditures. But, in most of the other

---

[177] Quoted from Shoup, *Public Finance*, p. 77; the inner quote comes from Fabricant, *op. cit.*, p. 101.

fields of public finance, the future seems to lie more with the Type 2 study, where an a priori structure of behavioral and definitional equations is first constructed, and then tested. This approach seems promising for further studies of effects of grants-in-aid; shifting and incidence; and effects of taxation on investment, on other business behavior, and on supply of labor; and other household reactions. The degree to which these models are truly tested will, no doubt, vary widely. Near one extreme, the model may do no more than establish a set of plausible relationships in the presence of a number of exogenous variables; and after real-life figures are fed into the model, the end data that it yields will be subject to an intuitive appraisal for reasonableness.[178] Near the other extreme lie techniques of testing that have been developed by econometricians, yielding conclusions which writers without specialized training in that field will have to take more or less on faith. When the experts differ (see Section II-C above), we shall have to suspend judgment until they resolve their differences.

How quickly we may expect results from Type 2 inquiries (a priori models) evidently depends not so much on development of further expertise in the field of public finance as on advances in econometric techniques for testing the model.

As to Type 1 studies—the evoking, or expanding, of parts of theoretical structures from facts that have been assembled for general purposes (e.g., as in *Statistics of Income*)—this is more a matter of theoretical public finance than it is of quantitative, or empirical, public finance. If it is observed that a tax on value added—of the consumption type—does not usually show the same base in national income data for any one year as does a tax on all labor income (it being recognized, nevertheless, that both taxes exempt either capital goods or the net return from capital goods), the result up to that point is a priori rather than quantitative. Such a result has obviously arisen in part from what might be called general observation of facts. This approach, helpful to the construction of a priori models needed in the Type 2 study, seems broadly applicable to all the sectors of public finance discussed above.

2. The quantitative questions posed will be more nearly completely specified than they have often been in the past. In the Type 2 studies, the models will be more surely closed. They still will not be general-equilibrium models in the Walrasian sense, since they will contain certain

---

[178] An illustration is the project being planned by Stephen Dresch and Carl S. Shoup, at the National Bureau, to estimate some of the distributive effects of federally financed general-purpose grants to states and localities.

exogenous variables; but, at least, they will not leave any of the important exogenous variables unmentioned (e.g., Where is the money to finance revenue-sharing coming from?). In the Type 3 studies (black-box studies) the phenomenon that is being described will be more broadly defined (see the critique in Section II-B above).

3. Field experiments of the type conducted by Mathematica, Inc. and the University of Wisconsin for ascertaining the effect of a negative income tax on work incentives [under the sponsorship of the Office of Economic Opportunity [179]] may be attempted on an increasing scale. Public finance is one field where the sponsors, i.e., governmental units, may have funds available on a large enough scale to make such studies possible. All kinds of intriguing research projects spring to mind, some of which would, most likely, be socially unacceptable: e.g., exempting from income tax for twenty years or so, certain executives and professional men, while taxing a control group of those types. This is a rough road, surely; and it may not prove fruitful—but who knows? Governments are continually providing us with changes in tax laws and expenditure programs that may be viewed for our purposes as experiments, the control group consisting of those in the time period before (or after) the change. But, here, the technique merges into that of Type 2 described above, with econometric tools.

4. The quantitative studies can be divided into those that deal with recorded, and observed, changes: for example, changes in prices or employment; and those that deal with things that are never a matter of record, e.g., the amount of excess burden. Research foundations will, we may hope, be sympathetic to the latter type of study, since it is quite unlikely to gain much financial support from governments.

5. As to outlets for future quantitative research, and sources of funds, we may assume that government departments will increase their efforts in the fields of taxation and government expenditure, given the increasing recognition in policy circles of the need for information. But what of the large private research or research-fostering organizations, e.g., the National Bureau of Economic Research and The Brookings Institution? Although they have in recent years spent considerable sums of money on this kind of research, and might therefore be expected to reduce their commitments in these areas, it seems to me that, again, the pressures are too great to allow this: pressures from policy-makers, the

[179] The project is being directed by Harold W. Watts, director of the University of Wisconsin Poverty Research Institute. For a summary of preliminary findings, see *Business Week* (Feb. 28, 1970), pp. 80–82.

public—and, of course, the academic world—to give quantitative answers, even if only approximate, to the urgent questions being posed in public finance. I am inclined to predict, therefore, that these organizations and others like them, here and abroad, will soon decide to reenter the public finance field on a fairly large scale, but with a somewhat different emphasis from that of the studies of the sixties, namely, an emphasis now on what has been termed above the closed model: a study of the effects of substituting one tax for another, of financing a stipulated increase in a certain type of expenditure by a stipulated tax, and so on.

No doubt there will be some delay in getting such studies under way if only because it will prove much more difficult to plan and staff closed-model studies than it was to do so with respect to studies each of which considered only one tax, or only one aspect of a tax, or but one type of government expenditure. More diverse talents and interests will have to be enlisted simultaneously for any one closed-model study. Moreover, even the simplest of such projects are likely to prove too much for any small group of individual scholars in a particular university (for example) on their own. The role of institutions such as the National Bureau and Brookings will for these reasons be, I think, even more important in the future than they have been in the past.

6. Outlets, if not financing, for quantitative public finance studies that are on a smaller scale than those envisaged in the preceding paragraph are now being provided by the scholarly journals in public finance and economics to a far greater extent than a few years ago. In the March, 1970, issue of the *National Tax Journal,* for example, three of the eleven articles included tests of hypotheses, and several of the others included formal models. At the same time, editors are willing to give space to conceptual or analytical articles in taxation and government expenditures, even those devoid of models. The June, 1970, issue of the *American Economic Review* contains four articles of this kind, and another with a model, but nonquantitative.

V. THE ROLE OF QUANTITATIVE STUDIES OF TAXATION OR GOVERNMENT EXPENDITURES IN THE FORMULATION OF POLICY

The questions to which this section is addressed are: What has been, and what will be, the role of quantitative research in taxation and governmental expenditures (excluding fiscal policy, and debt) in the formulation and implementation of policy? Specifically, what of the findings on: (1) distribution of taxation, transfer payments, and free government services by income classes, geographic groups, or other groups; (2) the shifting and incidence of taxes, transfer payments, and free government services; (3) the effects of taxation and subsidies or free services on growth (as shown by the effects on investment and other business-firm behavior), on the supply of labor, and on efficiency in the allocation of resources in the sense of avoiding unnecessary ("excess") loss of output ("loss of welfare" in the economist's terms)? We are also interested in comparative studies of tax systems and government expenditure systems from one country to another, or in one country over time, partly because of a search for "laws" of government-expenditure growth, and for measures of changes in efficiency in government.

As explained in the main body of this paper, quantitative work has apparently been concentrated, at least until recently, in the first two areas mentioned: distribution of taxation, transfer payments, and to a lesser degree, free government services, by income classes or geographic groups; and the shifting and incidence of particular taxes. (Almost no attention has been paid to the shifting and incidence of subsidies, and of free government services.) Let us speculate, first, what the impact of these studies has been on policy; and second, what it may be in the years ahead.

The influence of these distribution studies has not been very great if we are to judge by a comparison of what the tables for the United States drawn up in the 1930's and 1940's show in comparison with the tables for recent years. It might have been thought that the very uneven distribution of disposable income, coupled with the apparent finding that some 10 to 20 per cent of the income of poverty-level groups was being taken in taxation, would have stirred the community to action, diminishing that percentage. But this has not happened. Perhaps policy-makers recognized the logical fallacy that underlies a single tax-distribution table. (See Section II of this paper.) More likely, they turned their attention, quite properly, to means by which the disposable income of the lowest income-groups could be altered by changes in the tax system, and concluded that there were too many institutional difficulties in the way, including the need of local governments for the property tax, and the role of payroll taxes in enlisting support for the old-age and unemployment-compensation programs. Instead, an enhanced use of transfer payments to the poor has been employed. (The next step may well be a redistribution of free government services— police protection, fire protection, education—from the well-to-do to the poor.) It may be doubted, however, that this growth in transfer payments would have been much less if the tax distribution tables had never been constructed. All that was needed to stimulate the growth of transfer payments was the last column of such tables, showing disposable incomes by income classes. Whatever the reason for that degree of poverty, some action to mitigate it was evidently deemed desirable.

I would conjecture that in the future, the chief use of tax and transfer-payment distribution tables will be to indicate by how much the distribution of disposable income might be altered by postulated changes in that system. This implies the construction of alternative tables—not just one table—and the exercise will be only as useful as our knowledge of differential incidence allows it to be. Moreover, to be of greatest use for policy, these distribution tables must include something entirely new, i.e., some monetary expression (hopefully, in output terms, and if not that, in input terms) of the distribution of police protection, fire protection, education, and other government services that are not in the special category in which consumption of the service by one person neither impairs nor enhances the consumption of that same good by another person in the same group. It is in this direction, and in the increasing use of subsidy-type transfer payments (as opposed to transfer payments directly to households for general purposes) that there lies, in my view, the greatest promise for an important reduction in inequality of real total disposable income.[180]

But we encounter severe difficulties in this field of estimating the distribution of free government services, and they are not—as is commonly believed—primarily conceptual ones. To be sure, it will always be difficult to define units of output of a government service, and to place a money value on such a unit. But the real roadblock, at present, is the extreme reluctance of state and local government authorities, chiefly the officials of large cities, to release to public-finance scholars the data they already have, to say nothing of spending money to collect additional data. One can appreciate their reluctance, for the distributive issues involved in these studies are explosive, politically and socially. In a recent research project that I supervised, the police department of New York City proved courteous, but quite unresponsive, regarding requests for data other than those which had already appeared in the press, on deployment of police and police equipment among precincts.[181] While

[180] Shoup, *Public Finance*, pp. 581–588.

[181] See footnote 176 above. The Rand Corporation, at that time employed by the City to study its police operations (among other activities), proved likewise

there may be good short-term reasons for not making such information available (though I doubt that the criminal element scans many doctoral dissertations on microfilm for tips on where to operate), the long-run interests of the city officials, and, more to the point, of households and firms in the city, are crucially involved in the present shortsighted policy so common at the state and local level, with respect to data on distribution of certain state and local free governmental services.

Meanwhile, on the tax-transfer-payment front, more and more data are being made available, and studied—with the lamentable exception of subsidies, which seem to have been subject to very little serious quantitative analysis in terms of incidence; and, hence, also in terms of distribution by income or geographic classes (the maritime subsidies, for example). In other fields, the federal government has held for many years to an enlightened policy. Consider, for example, our Statistics of Income series. No other country in the world comes even close to the United States in the volume, quality, and skill in arrangement of data that mark this extraordinary series of quantitative information on taxation.[182] There have been times, particularly during the economy regime of Secretary of the Treasury Humphrey, in the 1950's, when Statistics of Income was threatened with reduction on a scale that would have left it distinctly second rate; but, happily, these pressures were successfully resisted. As a result, Congress and the executive branch have been able to compute the impact—if not the final incidence—of countless measures of tax reform, large and small, discarded or enacted, and of alternative programs to increase or decrease total federal tax revenues. In volume, and in influence on policy, these largely unpublished studies of impact distribution have almost surely been more influential in policy formulation than all the distribution studies published in scholarly journals and books. What we see in published form is but the tip of the iceberg, with respect to studies of distribution and other effects of proposed federal tax measures.

Many of the quantitative analyses made by the Office of Tax Analysis and the staff of the Joint Committee on Internal Revenue are

courteous but either unable to obtain, or relatively uninterested in obtaining, data on what appeared to Treviño-Westendarp and myself as the basic issues of equity and efficiency.

[182] Also, no other government, to my knowledge, possesses a tax analysis organization of the size and professional competence of the United States Treasury's Office of Tax Analysis, founded in 1938 under the title of Division of Tax Research.

of tax changes sufficiently small to allow the micro approach, where the use made of the increment, or decrement, in taxation can be neglected without incurring substantial error. Other branches of the federal government have produced a large amount of quantitative work on transfer payments (again, subsidies excepted), and, where transfer measures of large scope have been involved, a sophisticated macro approach has been used.[183]

But our optimism for future work on the distribution of income under differential tax, or transfer-payments, systems, or under different patterns of distributing certain free government services, cools considerably when we recall that these findings depend on the incidence assumptions that underlie them.

In taxation, quantitative research in incidence with respect to broad-based taxes has reached a most confusing stage. One who is not trained in econometrics may be made more pessimistic than he should be by the extent of disagreement among those econometricians who have worked on the incidence of the corporation income tax, or the effects of tax incentives in the federal income-tax law, but he has a right to be wary, particularly when the precise definition of what it is that they are measuring is not made clear.

Under these circumstances it seems premature to ask whether these types of empirical work on corporation tax incidence, so-called, will influence policy. They have not done so, and probably should not, in the present state of our knowledge. We still depend, in our own policy recommendations, I suspect, on simple little models that we carry around with us, unequipped with estimated coefficients.

Turning to transfer payments, we note that payments to households have been studied largely on an impact basis, without much consideration, for example, of how much of such payments is "shifted," i.e., lost, to landlords and others. As pointed out above, transfer payments to business firms in the form of subsidies have been studied hardly at all as to their incidence; although elementary supply-demand analysis suggests that any subsidy to a particular industry, like any tax on a particular industry, will go partly to consumers and partly to economic-rent recipients in that industry, according to the relative elasticities of supply and demand. As to free government services, even the impact distribu-

---

[183] See Benjamin Bridges, Jr., *Current Redistributional Effects of Old-Age Income Assurance Program.* Social Security Administration, Washington, D.C., 1968; and W. V. Vroman, *Macroeconomic Effects of Social Insurance on Aggregate Demand.* Social Security Administration, Washington, D.C., 1969.

tion remains to be determined; and then comes the task of a priori qualitative analysis of "shifting" possibilities; i.e., loss of benefit through operation of market forces.[184] Finally, perhaps, some quantitative analyses will emerge.[185]

Perhaps, the first step must be a sort of revolution in supply analysis. In a recent conversation with an economist who is in charge of planning for a large industrial concern, I inquired whether what he had learned from economic theory was of use to him in his present work. His reply was an emphatic affirmative with respect to the demand side (both micro and macro), and just as emphatic a negative with respect to supply. Not even the latest treatises on types of imperfect competition seem to have come close enough to reality, though it is possible that some of the recent work in decision-making will prove invaluable. Very likely, the basic trouble is that the economics profession grossly underrates the amount of effort needed to understand industry, and individual-firm, supply conditions in a complex industrial–service–raw-materials economy of two-hundred million persons, where the incorporated sector accounts for about three-quarters of the pretax profits of total business,[186] and a small number of corporations account for most of this.[187] Until we know far more than we do now about how the supply decisions are made in the large multiproduct corporations, we may not be able to construct the improved behavioral models that must be tested by an econometric appeal to the facts. (Let us recall that a monopoly has no supply schedule, only a cost schedule.) Economic research costing in the tens of millions of dollars, and extending over several decades, is probably what is needed, but we have neither the money nor the economists, as yet. Even a crude preliminary approach based on what we already know is so costly, running into the millions, and faces so great a risk of failure to get anywhere, that recent proposals along this line are, of necessity, being closely reexamined as to their feasibility.[188]

The next step may be, instead, to build even cruder, simpler models,

[184] Shoup, *Public Finance*, pp. 86–93.

[185] See footnote 176 above.

[186] Statistics of Income, 1965, Preliminary, *Corporation Income Tax Returns*, p. 2 (net income before tax, 1965, $74.2 billion); Statistics of Income, 1965, Preliminary, *United States Business Tax Returns: Sole Proprietorships and Partnerships*, p. 1 (net profit before individual income tax, $27.9 billion).

[187] See footnote 109 above.

[188] An example is the Bossons-Shoup tax-substitution general-equilibrium project described in the *Annual Report of the National Bureau of Economic Research for 1969*.

to learn more about what it is we need to know, before much progress can be made in quantitative differential-incidence for broad-based tax substitutions.

Meanwhile, whenever changes in micro taxes—certain excises, for example—are to occur, government or foundation resources should be mobilized to study price changes, without waiting for individual scholars to do what they can on their own. This remark applies particularly to state and local governments. It may also be applicable to small changes in the rate of the real estate tax.[189]

Policy formulation of something so specific and controversial as the recent federal investment credit may be influenced somewhat by empirical research; but in what direction, it is difficult to say, in view of the differences in the findings of various econometricians.[190]

More influential, I suspect, have been the case studies on effects of the income tax on the supply of labor, which—however lacking they may have been in model construction and statistical testing—have, at least, been reassuring in what they have failed to find, i.e., evidence that changes in tax rates have reduced labor effort considerably.

Quantitative work on the other topics covered in this paper has probably exerted little influence on policy. Time limitations prevent me from documenting this assertion. Comparative studies, to be sure, are apt to be of some influence, but more as ammunition to hold an already fortified position than as a means of deciding what policy to adopt.

It can be argued that nonquantitative public finance, i.e., public finance qualitative conclusions, or directional conclusions, have thus far been more influential in guiding policy than have the quantitative studies (apart from the numerous impact studies made within government agencies, referred to above). This state of affairs, if I have diagnosed it properly, may persist or change, or the entire question may vanish as we see more clearly the need for theoretical and empirical work to advance together. There is still plenty of room and need for both approaches—and, especially, for coordination between them.

[189] See the last three paragraphs in Section II-B above.
[190] See discussion of econometric studies in Section II-C (1) above.

DISCUSSION

Includes comments by Walter Heller, Chairman of the Board of Directors of the National Bureau of Economic Research and professor at the University of Minnesota, who was moderator of this session; and by James Buchanan, of the Virginia Polytechnic Institute, and Richard Musgrave, of Harvard University, who acted as program discussants; also, a reply to the discussants by Carl Shoup, of Columbia University. The recorded oral presentations were edited by, or with the cooperation of, the speakers. Remarks made during the open discussion period are not included.

Introductory Remarks by Walter Heller

I want to add my welcome to the fourth colloquium of the National Bureau's Fiftieth Anniversary series. I doubt that there's been such a gathering of the public finance clan since the occasion of the late Harold Grove's sixty-fifth birthday party. It is particularly appropriate that this colloquium should be dedicated to Harold's memory. Not only did he play an important role in the Bureau, but he devoted much of his professional lifetime to the stated purpose of these colloquia, namely, "to consider future research needs in light of present and anticipated policy problems." And he spawned no less than sixty-one Ph.D.'s during his career to help him with that quest!

By way of brief tribute to Harold's contributions and also as a reminder of how the public finance agenda has changed in the past thirty or forty years—and yet remains in many respects the same—I thought it might be interesting to quote just a few passages from his 1933–34 series of tax articles in the *New Republic,* which are classics. I divide these quotes into three categories.

The first was *love's labor lost:* "It now seems very clear," said he in 1934, "that we have reached the point where we can no longer afford the leaks and special privileges in our tax system which have been so abundantly demonstrated to exist. To mention only one of those leaks and privileges, what about the huge volume of tax-exempt interest? Second," he said in this connection, "those who fear the cumulative effect of federal and state income taxes should endorse the suggestion frequently made that the federal government give the taxpayer a credit against his federal tax for any income taxes that he pays the state." (I thought that the federal credit should have equal time with tax-sharing.) And then, "If the states wish to make the property tax more in accord with ability to pay, they can do so by making it apply to the 'net worth' of the taxpayer, including all assets, both tangible and intangible." A bold man was Harold.

The second category is *virtue rewarded*. In "Yachts Without Income" (what a great title!), he said the greatest single gap in the tax system was the unrestricted deductibility of capital losses, which permitted J. P. Morgan to have—you guessed it—yachts without income. Then he manfully put himself in the same class as J. P. Morgan by calling for an end to exemption of government salaries, including his own as a state university professor; the Congress obliged.

And then there is the third category, *the changing agenda*. He called for a tax on undistributed profits as well as a permanent excess profits tax. And he made the typical pre-Keynesian call for higher federal taxes to cut the deficit and sustain our money and credit. Now on the last point let me hasten to Harold Groves's defense with the following quote from an appeal by sixty-two members of the Johns Hopkins faculty to the U.S. Congress in 1932, calling for "the prompt adoption of a budget balanceable by vigorous retrenchment in the expenditures of all federal departments and by adequate emergency taxation."

* * *

James Buchanan: I suspect that the difficulties that Richard Musgrave and I face in discussing Carl Shoup's monograph were exceeded only by those which he faced in writing it. I don't know what Shoup's guidelines were, but I get the impression from reading the monograph that his heart wasn't really in it. We can perhaps appreciate why the National Bureau might have had an interest in a summary review of research as a part of its Fiftieth Anniversary. But in this age where we expose all hypocrisy, perhaps we should also acknowledge that research surveys are rarely of much value unless there is something other than a commemoration objective to be served. A more effective use of resources, I think, would have been to allow Carl Shoup to write a monograph on a topic of his own choosing. This would certainly have been more interesting to his discussants, and it might have served a commemorative purpose equally well.

But we are not here to dwell on what might have been. What we have before us is a monograph that purports to survey quantitative research in public finance over a half-century period. Now I like to think of a technically competent nonspecialist who might read this monograph.

And I should like to ask what impressions this nonspecialist would get about public finance and its development over the period from reading this monograph. In this connection I submit that the survey does provide a misleading and distorted picture of what has been and is happening in public finance. We have witnessed the transformation of what was a dull, unimaginative, extremely limited, and almost irrelevant subdiscipline into one of the most exciting areas in political economy. Yet this monograph fails to convey more than a trace of the revolution that has taken place. A nonspecialist reader would get the impression that public finance economists have continued to work with the same old problems, the only change being the employment of more and more sophisticated tools. Furthermore, he would have to conclude that, while some progress seems to have been made around the edges, nothing much has been accomplished by way of concrete results. And this nonspecialist reader of the survey would then surely not place a very high value on research prospects.

Now, what is the trouble? Is the over-all impression so misleading because Shoup has chosen to concentrate his attention on quantitative public finance research, which he juxtaposes against qualitative or theoretical research? It seems to me that this offers us only a small part of the answer. What has really happened in public finance is that our paradigms have been modified. We simply do not look at the subject matter of this subdiscipline in the same way that we did thirty years ago. And let us ask the question, what was public finance like thirty years ago? There were, of course, both positive and normative parts or elements of it. When I was a graduate student positive public finance consisted in analysis, almost exclusively nonquantitative, of the shifting and incidence of taxes. We tried to explain the effect on private economic behavior of individuals and firms that was exerted by the levy of taxes of different kinds and different magnitudes. And, as Shoup's monograph properly indicates, we're still trying to do this, but without having made much progress. In those days, normative public finance embodied the so-called "principles of taxation," a value-laden and extremely naive discussion about how taxes should be imposed. I think it is fair to say that public finance in those days was not political economy at all. The positive aspects were simply applied Marshallian price theory. Public finance did not embody a study of the public economy.

Today, by contrast, public finance is public economics. It is the economics of government, the study of the allocation of resources through public or collective decision processes. It is this incorporation of public choice that has made the dramatic difference in public finance. In one sense you could say that we put the word "public" back in the name. In another sense we could say that English-language public finance has made up a half-century lag that existed before World War II between its own level of sophistication and that of the Europeans. The contribution of Wicksell, Lindahl, and the Italians has now become a central part of the modern public finance tradition. And this change has come about through both normative and positive approaches. Such men as Musgrave, Bowen, and Samuelson showed us how welfare conditions for public sector allocations could be derived from individual evaluations. Alongside this, such men as Kenneth Arrow, Duncan Black, and Anthony Downs begin to show us the positive results of attempts to combine individual evaluations into collective outcome. Surprising as that may seem to us here today, public finance economists have come to look on governments as being made up of ordinary men only within the past two decades. Only within those two decades has a serious analysis of the actual workings of the bureaucratic process been commenced by such people as Gordon Tullock, Anthony Downs, Roland McKean, William Niskanen, and others. I think we have indeed come a long, long way; so far, in fact, that the study of public economy now includes as only one part, and a relatively small part at that, the traditional problems of tax shifting and incidence. It therefore seems to me little wonder that Shoup's summary survey should be somewhat misleading in its concentration on what has now come to be a small part of a much larger and more important subject. Most of you who know my own approach to public finance could have predicted this to be my general response. I have summarized it here because there are, or so it seems to me, quite important implications for public finance research. I think we have no more than scratched the surface of investigation into just how governmental processes do, in fact, work. I think there is a veritable mine to be exploited here, and we can point to only a handful of empirical contributions. Let me mention just one or two. How are budgets actually made? Surely the Davis-Dempster-Wildavsky results cannot be ignored when people start asking that question. How do regulatory commissions actually work? The research efforts of George Stigler and his cohorts must remove some of the naiveté from some of the people who ask that question. We need hard-headed empirical research into the workings of every constitutional or legislative assembly, court, bureau, agency, commission, and committee of every level of government in the land.

The research that I'm calling for is empirical and quantitative, but it does not require complex or complicated techniques, and it will scarcely excite the young economist who has a set of fancy tools and no ready-made places to apply them. The research tools needed are the simple motivational assumptions that the economist carries around with him along with a hard-headed critical understanding of the way that actual and political collective-decision institutions function. We have too long neglected institutional considerations. I would personally like to see far more institutional analysis reintroduced into public finance and into economics generally. And I was a little impressed by Shoup's remarks where he called for research on the workings of the tobacco industry and the multiproduct corporations. But neither in his remarks nor in his monograph did he call for research into the way the government works and the way bureaus work. I see Roy Blough here, and I am frankly a little embarrassed when I think back to my reactions to his book *The Federal Taxing Process*. I remember that, before I saw the light, my initial reaction to that book was negative, but that is the type of research that we need.

What could be expected as the effects of such research even if it should be undertaken and completed along precisely the lines that I suggested? I think that we must hold fast to the view that research results ultimately affect men's attitudes toward policy. If men come to understand more about how bureaucracy actually works, perhaps they will tend to assign to bureaucracy only those tasks that it can perform with reasonable effectiveness. Even more importantly, once a better institutional understanding is accomplished, the emphasis can then be placed on institutional innovations which are designed to foster increasing bureaucratic efficiency.

It seems to me that modern economists are prone to take either one of two routes in their research. The larger group undertakes research in any subject provided only that the data are such as to allow them to apply their econometric techniques. Karl Brunner calls them "econometrarians." This group tends to be far more interested in applications of technique than in any substantive results that might emerge. The smaller group will undertake research in the manipulation of models whose assumptions sometimes remove them too far from the world of reality. Of the two, I suppose it is clear that my prejudice is inclined toward the latter group, but I feel a little guilty sometimes because I feel strongly that the most productive research lies somewhere between these two poles. We need empirically based and empirically informed research into the theory of both actual and potential institutional structures. Let me give you a simple example. We do not need elaborate econometrics to explain why hospital costs are soaring under medicare. We do need a rudimentary understanding of the institutional structure of the hospital, and understanding of the decision processes that are involved, and of the reward-punishment structure confronted by those persons who must make the relevant decisions. It's only when we have such an under-standing that the institutional innovations that are essential to resolve this cost-increase phenomenon could be expected to be forthcoming.

Of course, each of us would have his own favorite agenda for re-search, and it is not to be expected that mine would parallel that of Carl Shoup. Nonetheless, I submit that the agenda that I have just alluded to does offer a far more exciting horizon to the young scholar and to the research entrepreneur in the foundation than the somewhat tired topics in traditional public finance that Shoup has perhaps overemphasized. Each man should, of course, be encouraged to do his own thing, and I don't object to further research along the lines which Shoup has called for. My complaint is really not that he has led us down a false path—not at all. It is rather that he has failed to suggest that there are more inter-esting alternative routes to follow in what we may legitimately label public finance research.

Walter Heller: *Thank you very much, Jim. You did exactly what a discussant should do—injected some controversy, some substance, some positive suggestions, offended young economists, offended old public finance men, and even threw a few crumbs to us old institutionalists.*

Richard Musgrave: I am happy to follow the example of our other speakers in beginning with a few words about Harold Groves. Shortly before he died, I gave a lecture at Wisconsin which he attended. I took the opportunity then to say why I have admired him so much. It was his positive and courageous approach to the solution of public policy problems—the kind of attitude which expressed his midwestern pro-gressive faith that ultimately things can be done reasonably. It was the same spirit that I admire so much in my teacher, Alvin Hansen, and I think there is not enough left of it today. I told Harold that I thought that he and Hansen symbolized what, as someone with a European background, I had come to think of admiringly as an American intel-lectual. Of late, too many American intellectuals have become European intellectuals, which, I fear, has been a dubious gain.

Now let me say a word about what should be included in public finance. Carl noted in his introduction that he did leave out fiscal policy, and that he considered certain aspects of cost-benefit analysis as marginal. It is, of course, true that the macroeconomics of fiscal policy and their methodology fit into a different course than the microeconomics of, say, tax incidence. But we may be going too far toward ruling out all macro aspects. When I was a graduate student, probably a decade before James Buchanan, I was taught that the only function of taxes was to be a deflationary factor in the economy, and at that time the public finance problem was seen in purely macro terms. Since then the macro aspects have come to be practically eliminated. But as Shoup points out, we need a general equilibrium approach to many of these problems, and this brings the macro aspects back into the fold.

But the very scope of the public finance field makes it increasingly difficult to hold all its facets together. Why should a student who wants to study cost-benefit analysis be interested equally in corporation tax depreciation or in the stabilization aspects of fiscal policy? This is something which all of us who teach the field encounter increasingly. One might well say that the only unique aspect of the economics of public finance—that is, genuine public finance—is the theory of social goods, normative and positive. This is the essence of public finance as a separate discipline, and all the rest is the application of various tools of economic analysis to one or another aspect of fiscal operations. But even with this narrow definition, the economics of public finance, once an obscure corner of the science, is rapidly coming to be a central subject of economic theory, as it is now being taught.

So much for the general problem of staking out the field. Let me go on and say a word about methodology, because this is one of the most interesting aspects of the problem which Carl Shoup has discussed. Certainly, theorizing is not enough. There is a desperate need for empirical work. In most controversial issues of tax incidence and expenditure effects there can be a variety of a priori theoretical hypotheses which are not offhand unreasonable. For instance, you can convince yourself of a theory of the firm which says that the corporation tax is not shifted, or of one which says that it is shifted. The answer has to be found in empirical work. This need is well illustrated by the studies of tax burden distribution which Shoup discussed at some length and which I have been working on at various stages, following up the earlier work of Tarasov and Colm. The crux of these studies lies in the hypotheses made regarding the incidence of corporation and property taxes. These are the two strategic factors, and until we have good empirical evidence on them, the results are hypothetical. To get further, we must tackle this empirical job.

Moreover, as Carl points out, we must begin to deal with these problems in terms of a general equilibrium analysis. It is important, as he puts it, to consider them in terms of closed systems. This is surely right. If we ask what happens if this tax is imposed or if that tax is repealed, one must take into account the inflationary or deflationary effects. To disregard them would not be a very meaningful way of posing the question. So one should think of incidence in terms of differential effects. I disagree with Buchanan that incidence is a tired subject. To be sure, it is extremely interesting to think about how the political mechanism can be designed to lead to a more meaningful relationship between tax policy and expenditure policy. I quite agree with that. But the fact of the matter is that taxes are largely determined and set independent of expenditures, and that the benefit theory, beautiful though it is, is not easily applied. Taxes are not voluntary payments, nor need they stay put with the payee. Knowing what their incidence is thus becomes extremely important. It is especially important because our society must increasingly face the issue of income and welfare distribution, an issue which, in my judgment, is perhaps more serious than any other aspect of public policy.

Yet, the design of the distribution problem is made difficult by our lack of knowledge regarding differential incidence. The usual studies of tax burden distribution are subject to the criticism that they look at the absolute burden of particular taxes rather than at differential incidence. By assuming pretax income to be unaffected, one may compare a particular tax with a standard, such as a proportional income tax, and show the differential. This, however, is really cheating because it does not produce a solid general equilibrium analysis. As Prest pointed out, you cannot get around the difficulty by assuming that the distribution of income before tax is independent of the tax system. But to construct a general equilibrium model of the Walrasian type which includes not only all relative product and factor prices but also their relationship to the size distribution of income is an enormous, if not impossible, task.

Looking back over the decades, I am impressed with the lack of simplifying genius in the field of microeconomics, such as Wicksell and Keynes have produced in the field of macroeconomics. Ricardo did have a beautiful system which gave the key to incidence, but, as Schumpeter pointed out, its only difficulty was that it was all wrong. There has been Walras and his splendid system of $n - 1$ equations, a system which is right by definition but does not get us anywhere in solving practical incidence issues. What is needed is a breakthrough in terms of a manageable system of relative product and factor prices and their relative income distribution, a system which, one hopes, has fewer than 4,999 equations and can yield meaningful results.

This raises the problem of econometric models. These models involve a general equilibrium approach, but partial equilibrium aspects must be understood to construct them. The initial question to be considered is: How do the tax variables enter the consumption function? How do they enter the dividend function? How do they enter the investment function? It would be interesting to take the various models (Brookings, Wharton, Federal Reserve/MIT, D.R.I., etc.) and see just how the fiscal variables are inserted into these various expenditure functions, and what this implies regarding the effects of changes in fiscal parameters. Study of micro responses to fiscal variables thus comes first, because it is needed to determine how they enter into the model. Even though partial equilibrium analysis is not enough, it is needed as a first stepping stone toward a meaningful general equilibrium model.

Now I come to the most difficult and, in a way, the most important part of the problem; that is, the contribution to be expected from econometrics. I believe that this contribution is vital. Notwithstanding my primary interest in the normative theory of social goods, I know that governmental action must involve compulsion and is thus bound to induce responses in the private sector. The nature of these responses, therefore, must be known if government behavior is to be efficient. Theorizing alone is not enough and finding the answers stands and falls with the success of econometrics. The empirical science of public finance, we might as well admit, is largely an application of econometrics. The specialized aspects of public finance are only a minor part of the problem.

What type of econometric model should be used for public finance analysis? We appear to be at a point where some disillusionment is setting in among econometricians as to the usefulness of very large models. If so, it would be unfortunate for researchers in public finance to move toward their use. Moreover, the kinds of questions which these researchers must ask are much more difficult to answer by econometric models than the questions which the macroeconomists have asked. Given a large model with substantial lags and many exogenous variables, it does not appear too difficult to determine what will happen to GNP next year. Even though models may differ greatly in detail, they cannot very easily miss, especially if GNP keeps going up anyway. But the outcome is much less certain if one wishes to determine what happens if we change the corporation tax rate, or the property tax rate, or even the income tax rate, or if we adjust this or that item of government expenditure. If you ask these selective questions, the different models will give strikingly different answers. This is the case because tremendous weight is now placed on the structural nature of particular equations, the specific design of which determines the multiplicand generated by a particular policy measure. Since these particular equations—say, the investment equation—differ greatly in the different models, it is not surprising that we get very different results.

I am not saying this to discredit econometric work. I believe that this is where the future lies. But to improve matters, much more work has to be done on how the tax variables should be fitted into the basic functions. The recent debate over the nature of the investment function was most helpful, and Jorgenson—although he seems to have lost the now mythical battle at the Brookings conference—made a major contribution in trying to design a microeconomically meaningful investment function. This was an important step forward, but much more work will have to be done before the effects of selective policy changes can be generally predicted.

For purposes of incidence analysis, we must also take these macro-models and link them to the problem of income distribution. This surely is going to be a tremendously difficult task. Unfortunately, we cannot be satisfied any more (as was Ricardo) with studying the effects of various measures on factor shares. We are interested in their effects on the size distribution of income, presenting a whole array of problems which do not even appear in these models. Before the distributional dimension can be incorporated into the large models, I think that it would be well to deal with much smaller models in which one can experiment with these problems.

One of the great difficulties for econometrics in fiscal research is that, for so many problems, we have to use time-series analysis. Here we must recognize that, as I should well know, the fiscal variables (e.g., corporate tax rates) tend to be highly collinear with everything else. Tax receipts go up when the buoyancy of the economy goes up and go down when buoyancy goes down. And when both tax receipts and expenditures go up, you have an apparently insoluble problem of collinearity. As a consumer rather than producer of econometric tools, I think that we must develop more sensitive instruments to deal with collinearity if we are to get results in this field.

Now let me comment briefly on large versus small projects. Carl's emphasis has been on the need for large projects, but I would say, as did the chairman, let the flowers bloom. There is a place for everything. Important contributions have come from small-scale projects, as, for instance, Carl Shoup's work on the allocation of police effort in New York City, Dale Jorgenson's work, and many other cases. One can also think of large projects which proved extremely useful—for instance, Joe Pechman's income tax model. So, it seems to me that there is a place for everything. In research, as in other connections, it is good investment portfolio behavior to spread risks. When one can have a hundred small projects or one large project, one has to be pretty sure that the payoff on the large project is going to have a high probability of return. But surely there is room for both.

Finally, just a word with regard to what I think are some of the most important problems to work on. In reading the *New York Times* today, I learned that the administration may be thinking of an expanded revenue-sharing plan, not on a $4 or $5 billion but on a $10 or $15 billion scale. It seems to me that we are embarrassingly unprepared to deal with this problem. As I see it, the most important problem to be resolved at this point is to find some way of measuring not only the fiscal capacities but also the fiscal needs of the various jurisdictions. This is a difficult and messy issue, but I think it is one of the most important problems to be tackled.

Another issue which is most important from a current point of view concerns the incentive effects of the negative income tax. This is a field where, as Carl mentioned, some experimentation has taken place. While it appears that the experiment has not been very successful, this is certainly an area where work need be done. A third area of increasing interest, like it or not, is the possibility of substituting a value-added tax for the corporation income tax or other taxes. To do this, we need some greatly simplified macromodels containing the relationships most important for this purpose but cutting out excessive details. Some work of that sort would be most helpful, particularly if available by the time of Congressional consideration. The analysis of tax incidence, especially for the corporation tax and property tax, is something that has to be continued. I agree with my critics that, in order to get at the corporation tax problem, a more disaggregated model is needed and one which introduces some explicit assumptions about the pricing behavior of firms. The difficulty is that, to do a good job, detailed information is required on costs and prices, that products have to be defined over time, and so forth. Basic data work may have to be undertaken before much estimating can be done. As Buchanan suggests, the analysis of bureaucracy, of how government works, is also a challenging and important problem. Perhaps one of the best things in our field is that there is great variety, with different people interested in different things. The best bet, I believe, is that good researchers, left to their own interests, will find the most promising problems. Research foundations should respond to these interests, rather than guide them.

Walter Heller: *Thank you, Dick, for a fascinating discussion. You did just what a second discussant should do, namely, disagree with both the speaker and the first discussant. The agenda of unfinished business gets longer and longer. I should also note that there were some very good practical inferences that can be drawn from what you said, namely, that Wilbur Mills and John Byrnes can wait until they have the results of your analysis before they change their opposition to revenue sharing. I imagine that will be rather reassuring to them. Of course, the real question is, will the Congress wait, will it heed?*

Now before we turn to defenders of econometrics and the 5,000-equation models, we should give our initial speaker a chance to comment on some of the comments that have been made. Then also, Jim, if you want to say something in response to what Dick has said I think we might do that before opening the meeting to discussion from the floor.

Reply by Carl Shoup: I'll try to be brief, although Professor Buchanan's remarks were all so quotable I hardly know where to begin. But at any rate, it does seem to me it's a great pity that Jim wasn't born forty years earlier, and also Gordon Tullock and his other coworkers, so that by now there would have been a big body of empirical research on their special interests for me to survey when I wrote my paper. But since fate decreed otherwise, there wasn't really very much that could be said on that score.

As to what should be covered in my paper, that, of course, is partly a matter of choice, partly a matter of assigning relative importance. I'm inclined to agree with Dick Musgrave, if I heard him correctly, that shifting and incidence are not really tired topics. Perhaps Jim is tired of them—I can understand that. We all get in that mood occasionally. But there is still more to be said in these fields and I'm a little disappointed that Buchanan himself wasn't excited about extending the field of analysis into government services, subsidies, and so on. What it seems to come down to is that there's still plenty of work for all of us to do. I can't associate myself with Buchanan's value scale with respect to the topics for research in public finance, but there's no reason why he should have to associate himself with mine.

As to the comments that Professor Musgrave made, I find myself pretty much in agreement with him, except it is a provocative thought that we haven't had any genius in this field of microeconomics that might be compared with Ricardo, Wicksell, and Keynes in macroeconomics. I suppose Dick would be willing to put Cournot in that category. To be sure, that was a long time ago. Cournot gave us the framework, we just haven't moved very far from his base—that's the trouble. But perhaps this field is not one that calls for genius—maybe it just calls for a lot of hard work from all of us. The task is, as I suggested, even bigger than we yet appreciate. It is to find out how firms work and what they do.

Not knowing much about it I can speak clearly and say that I'm in general sympathy with the idea of small models—how small, of course, is another matter. They should presumably be made small in a way that allows them to grow. I agree that the ultimate goal is the use of large models, sooner or later. But we risk a great deal by attempting to put too much into one large project—the large model. That was not what I meant when speaking of the large amounts of time and effort now needed; what I want to suggest, instead, is that for the really detailed work of finding out what goes on in the business firms of the world (micro work), we need far more time and more millions of dollars than we yet appreciate. Until we do appreciate that we will remain pretty much where we are.

As to current topics of pressing interest, I'm inclined to think that value-added taxation is going to be discussed, but its chief interest for us is not as a substitute for corporate income tax but as part of a general reform of the federal tax structure, along with a couple of other tax measures, notably a net worth tax and a progressive-rate spendings tax. The value-added tax, if it is needed at all, is needed as a chief instrument for counter-cycle policy, for which I think income tax has shown itself pretty well ineffective, I'm sorry to say. That's quite a change in my point of view from four or five years ago. The value-added tax is certainly a lively subject for discussion, but we should think of it in a much broader framework. Thank you.

James Buchanan: *Thank you, Carl. I want to comment by saying I withdraw the word "tired."*

Closing Remarks by Walter Heller

One thing that we can all see in the vast unfinished business of research in taxation and public expenditure is that Justice Felix Frankfurter was speaking the truth when he prefaced his remarks in a complex income tax case many years ago by quoting Edmund Burke, to the effect that "taxation, like love, is not founded wholly on reason." That certainly is still true today. By the way, in his dissent in that particular tax case, he went on to say, "This is a plain, unvarnished, luscious bonanza of a windfall." We can stand a little more of that kind of plain speaking in Washington even now.